Clubbed
Class

Jon Ronson

Clubbed Class

PAVILION

For Elaine

First published in Great Britain in 1994 by
PAVILION BOOKS LIMITED
26 Upper Ground, London SE1 9PD
Copyright © Jon Ronson 1994

The moral right of the author has been asserted.
Designed by Cole design unit

A CIP catalogue record for this book is available
from the British Library.

ISBN 1 85793 3206

Phototypeset in 10/12^{1}/$_{2}$pt Meridien by Intype
Printed and bound in Great Britain by
Hartnolls Ltd, Bodmin, Cornwall

2 4 6 8 10 9 7 5 3 1

This book may be ordered by post direct from
the publisher. Please contact the Marketing
Department. But try your bookshop first.

Contents

1

The skies above Johannesburg, 3.00 p.m., Friday. We're bouncing up and down in a tiny ten-seater plane heading towards Sun City – Elizabeth, a rich white from Jo'burg's elegant Hyde Park district, Mary, a young, rich, black girl from Zimbabwe, and me, on our way to gamble and hob-nob with the glitterati and swim in the fake waves of the authentically African Palace Of The Lost City where we'll be greeted by authentic Africans in authentic head gear, calling us 'master', the whole thing engineered by a top Hollywood designer for £200 a night.

And a strange and worryingly likable hotel concept it is: a fake Africa for the well-to-do, slap bang in the middle of the genuine article, with waterfalls and game parks and big stone elephants and flowing streams and savannas and all, walled and patrolled by armed guards eagerly halting spoilsport natives disinclined to call you 'master' from sneaking in and spoiling the fun.

Weird, but oddly comforting: not unlike, say, a Manchester-based Moss Side World where everyone says 'Eh up, chuck' and gives you free eccles cakes, or, maybe, a Compton-located South Central LA Experience where festive Negroes called Chicken George sing 'Swing Low, Sweet Chariot' while cheerfully hammering steel girders into the ground.

'Journalist eh?' says Elizabeth moments after I've sat down. 'Let me tell you something about the ANC. They're a CIA-funded conspiracy. My brother used to say that if you get rid of America and . . . um . . . another country which he hated, I can't remember which it is now . . . anyway, if you get rid of these two countries, then there'd be no war.' And she slams her hand on the table.

But not to worry, for we are on our way to the southern hemisphere's very own Sodom and Gomorrah, where an authentic volcano erupts every hour on the hour, and the waiters quiver on their knees, like ancient tribal people do when they incur the wrath of the gods. And all hail to Sun City supremo Sol Kersner for creating this Xanadu where before stood only

3

scrubland. If Kubla Khan had married Fredo Corleone, moved to South Africa and got him pregnant, the resulting child would resemble Sol Kersner. Sol: the hotelier, the statesman.

Not even Mandela himself has managed to unite the Boers, Bophuthatswana's great dictator Lucas Mangope, the ANC, the far right and the National Party to a common goal, but Sol has. He understands that the needs of his people are simple: a three-hundred-and-fifty-bedroom luxury hotel, complete with authentic African water-slides dug out of the mountain, a surf beach with golden sands, a reasonably priced massage service (the masseurs themselves are more than happy to give you an extra special 'down below' option for a small supplementary charge), and, most of all, the 'Treasure Temple', five hundred slot machines whirring twenty-four hours a day, benevolently accepting the sacrifices of worshippers to this magnificent Temple of Mammon.

———

Not long before I left for South Africa, I read in the papers that Santa Claus had been done for child molestation three streets down from where I live. The little boy in question was out of his mother's sight for a moment when Father Christmas jumped out from behind the bushes and brutalized the poor wretch.

I'd been wanting to do some spectacularly glamorous international travel for a while, and when things were this rotten in my neighbourhood (this is a man, mind you, whose job description includes making an annual moral assessment on whether *we've* been naughty or nice, the bastard), then it was time to get the hell out and discover a place where everyone is nice to each other and says urbane and scintillating things like in David Niven movies.

I wanted to sip cocktails in a place where the only crimes are the fun white-collar crimes of major fraud, tax evasion, insider-trading, dazzling, glittering sexual perversions, and the odd 'Rich Pig Hippy Cult Slaying' or 'All-American College Kid With Secret Heroin Problem Bludgeons The Parents For The Inheritance And Makes It Look Like The SLA Did It' to add some colour to the proceedings.

———

It had been brewing for a while, long before Santa turned against us, long before he brought a whole new meaning to the words: 'You better watch out, You better not cry, You better not shout . . .' No. Nowadays, whenever I read about the lives of the rich and dazzling, about Mao Zedong (flesh-eating teen orgies), J. Edgar Hoover (girls' dresses, call me 'Mimi'), Michael Jackson (we'll get you, Mr Weird Nose) and on and on, I found myself experiencing a growing, curiously overpowering envy, an avaricious urge to attend their parties.

Sadly, of course, all this opulence has its price, and it was a price that I could not afford. Don't get me wrong: I can handle the degradation of kowtowing to the powerful and corrupt and stupid. I can handle the betrayal of my class: the whole point of *being* lower-middle class is that you ultimately betray it, one way or another. That's the thing about my people – every other social grouping has an easily definable culture to be proud of. The working classes have tin baths, scurvy and being everywhere in chains. The upper classes have *Tatler*, the Ritz, and auto-asphyxiation. All *we've* got are sparkling wine and the Lake District. So I must stress, the price that I could not afford is not a metaphoric price, it is a wholly financial one.

Let me explain. My reckless grappling for a ticket into High Society is an ingrained thing: I spent many of my child-hood years being dragged on family outings to the Changing of the Guard, the Boat Race and the Royal Tournament. 'Look at Prince Edward,' my father would yell. 'Why can't you have that poise? Look at the Royal Signals White Helmet Infantry Division. Wouldn't you like to be in charge of them one day?'

And I did look: thirty of them riding around in a big *Keystone Cops*-esque pyramid on top of one motorbike to the strains of the Royal Navy Massed Bands doing 'Hey Jude'. I remember being, even at the age of six, a tad uneasy about how this – admittedly very dazzling – accomplishment could possibly be put to effective use in a combat situation. But, spurred along by the rampant patriotism all around me, I acknowledged that we could, at a push, find ourselves in a war-torn environment with only one Honda.

These were halcyon, pre-Fergiegate, pre-Camillagate, pre-

Di-falling-downstairsgate days, when it was possible for we Brits to celebrate our Greatness, because there was Greatness to be found.

Nowadays, of course, the spirit of the Royal Tournament is geared primarily to the tourists. (We have to *live* here! You can't pull the wool over *our* eyes!) A celebration of past Naval victories – Gibraltar 1704, Copenhagen 1801 (you can imagine the Battle for Copenhagen – a couple of mellow Danes saying 'Yeah, take it') – is, at best, an embarrassingly inappropriate delineation of our fast dwindling national vitality. It's all just too grand for the country we now live in. Nowadays, the tourists are being excited and patriotic on our behalf, while we sit at home terrified to go out for fear of being cut down in our prime by a three-year-old crack addict with an uzi. It was therefore indisputable that if I wanted to sample the high life I'd have to travel away from these shores to a new land where the rich and powerful still know how to have a good time at the expense of penniless mendicants like me.

_____

Consequently, I am Sol Kersner's guest today. This book (provisional title: *High Class, Affordable Prices – The Sun King Shines On*), was a 'fascinating concept', his people said, and they've provided the plane, the champagne, all the hot-air-balloon-rides I've ever dreamt of (which – I must admit – is no hot-air-balloon-rides whatsoever), golf, and on and on.

And I accepted! I accepted! I mean – hell – I'd done my bit in the struggle against apartheid, of which Sol was Public Enemy Number One (even though Sun City was the one place under the regime where Afrikaner men were free to copulate with black women without being obliged to shop them to the security forces during the post-coital cigarette; something which, you'll agree, is rather a downer on a first date).

In fact, just last week I was invited to a whites only, pre-election 'Viva Mandela' party in the bar of an expensive London hotel. I'm not certain that the ticket actually specified 'No Blacks' – in fact I doubt it, given the circumstances – but there you go: it just so happened that this was one of those expensive London hotels where you don't get many blacks. (I once asked a Boer white supremacist living in London why he hated the British so much, and he replied: 'Mr Pot, say hello to Mr Kettle.')

It was a riotous night. Drinks were flying, people were doing the 'Free Nelson Mandela Cha Cha Cha' through the tables. Somebody even started mournfully crooning: 'Zimbaaaabwe Zimbaaaabwe Rhodesia/Mugabeeee . . .' But it was fine, because we all knew what he was on about. I spent the evening dreading the moment when somebody suggested we play ANC charades, because I hadn't the foggiest how I was going to act out Joe Slovo (although Winnie Mandela is a piece of piss. All I needed was a baseball bat and a large group of small boys).

And I *deserved* to celebrate. I've danced spiritedly to 'Free Nelson Mandela' at the Cardiff High School sixth-form disco. I've marched up and down Kensington High Street yelling 'Viva Mandela!' at the little old ladies trying to buy their fruit and veg on a Saturday afternoon. (And, for all we knew, Pik Botha *may* have been window shopping for leather trousers at Ken Market that day: he *may* have glanced behind him, seen me, and gone, 'Oh fuck! Jon's *right*! What we need *is* a great big melting pot.')

It's been tough, the last few years, the struggle being my life, and I feel no guilt. This is the new South Africa where I can check into Sun City and get called 'master' and nobody is allowed to sniff or get tetchy. International tetchiness is a thing of the past, now that South Africa is open for business.

———

As a reserve tactic, I had also approached a 'First Class Safari Outfit' called Jungle Tours, telling them I was writing an article on the rhapsody and affordability of lion gazing, and they immediately (really fast – called back the next day) offered me a ticket for a fun, three week, 'easy' journey through Zimbabwe.

And I wasn't kidding myself. I guessed the trip would include a certain amount of strenuousness – I'd probably have to do *some* trekking in dusty locations, maybe even a night or

———

two in one of those big tents with carpets hanging off the wall. But I could handle all that.

I spoke to my outdoor-minded friends who enthusiastically recounted, with doomy relish (a tone of voice they save for the few opportunities they get to scare indoor types like me), tales of friends of friends of friends, first-timer safari virgins having to climb trees to elude oncoming irate rhinos, being ripped to shreds by baboons.

'Actually "shreds"?' I inquired. 'Did your friends actually mention the word "shreds"?'

'Shreds,' they replied, with gusto (as if being ripped to shreds would be an appropriate retribution for the fact that I've spent my life dining out and watching TV instead of swinging across waterfalls like they'd been doing.)

'Just don't throw the fruit back at them. That's the key to survival.'

'I suppose that they're as frightened of us as we are as them,' I said.

'Don't be ridiculous,' they replied. 'We're not frightened of them.'

'What if there're no trees to climb?' I said.

'Run in a zig-zag,' they replied. 'And when you're camping in the bush, keep the sleeping bag over your head.'

But Jungle Tours were a different kettle of fish, they told me. They were 'High Class'. A night at the Waldorf Astoria cocktail bar with a couple of affable rhinos thrown into the landscape. London, but hotter and with better traffic control. *White Hunter, Black Heart*. John Huston. Longleat without the ice-cream stalls. A *Face* Zimbabwe fashion spread. Meryl Streep going, 'I arm fraam Arrrfrica.' The whites of their eyes. And so on.

And then all I can do is hope for the best. There is a certain amount of mileage to be gained from being a slavishly obsequious journo, writing a glowing and appallingly humble portrait of whatever hotel is willing to put me up.

And after that? Who knows. I'm young, cheap, easy to please and thrilled at the prospect of sipping aperitifs in cornucopian African resorts surrounded by majestic wild creatures that I can gaze at from the hotel window, while dancing indigenous locals make me recognize salient truths about myself. It will be humbling – yet genially first class – which is the best sort of humbling.

––––

People in South Africa talk about South Africa, and that's all. You're sitting in a taxi and you say: 'Lovely day,' (a dumb statement to make in the middle of an arid continent, admittedly) or 'How's business?' or 'Don't run over that pigeon,' and they'll grunt and gaze disinterestedly through the cracks in the windscreen. But if you ask them whether they think Mandela will form a coalition with de Klerk, you may as well take the afternoon off. This is understandable of course. South African politics are inalienably linked with day-to-day life: an unpopular law is passed in the morning, and, by lunchtime, someone has placed a blazing tyre around your neck. This is interactive politics at its most vibrant.

So, up here in the plane, Elizabeth and I speak about the Soweto Uprising of 1976: 'Of *course* we had to shoot the children. They're the *dangerous* ones. It's the eight- and nine-year-olds who are doing all the killings. That's why Mandela wants to lower the voting age to fourteen. All the ANC terrorists are *children.*'

And we speak about the whites: 'We're in terrible danger right now, and we mustn't forget that. We're destroying ourselves by being so bloody understanding.' And she tuts and shakes her head.

––––

But things are changing today, right underneath the plane. The whites are fighting back. The far-right AWB, under the leadership of celebrated philanderer Eugene Terre'Blanche, has called in thousands of armed supporters – 'farmers turned cowboys' mutters Mary – and has declared the Bophuthatswanian homeland a 'whites only area'. They've been threatening rivers of blood for ages now, unless the election is called off, unless Mandela promises not to redistribute their farmland and wealth. And this could be their day.

Bophuthatswana's president, Lucas Mangope (who it

––––

seems also opposes the election for equally – if not more – avaricious reasons: home rule would mean an immediate relinquishment of his glittering lifestyle, his helicopters and country residences) has fled his home. Some say he's hiding out in Sun City, in room 238 of the Cascade Hotel. (Ah! for the safety and fastidiously created tranquillity of Sun City, where even Lucas Mangope can hide out in an exquisitely placid Africa where people like Mangope don't exist. Well, that's the theory anyway, but the reality is somewhat more worrying: the Bophuthatswanian people hate Mangope, and the vast majority of Sun City's staff are Bophuthatswanian.)

Down below, the AWB are patrolling the area near the hotel, shooting the locals. Just now, three AWB members were lying on the ground by a car in nearby Mmabatho, pleading, 'Just get us a fucking ambulance, I beg you,' to the international news crews. And a Bophuthatswanian soldier shot them in the head.

———

Up here on the plane, drinking complimentary champagne, Elizabeth tells me how her country's had such a terrible press: 'I used to live in England, and I didn't know *any* blacks. Now I know *many* blacks. My maid, her family. And you grow a real close attachment to them. When they get sick, you don't throw them out of the house. You make them better.'

And then she says, 'Let's not get rose tinted here. Let's remember that the blacks still burn witches. Let's remember that the people who are going to vote in this election still burn witches.'

Whenever she says the word 'black', she whispers it under her hand, so that Mary doesn't hear. While all this is happening, the airline steward is walking up the aisle, giving out complimentary newspapers. He hands one to Elizabeth, one to me, grunts at Mary, and walks on. Mary looks crestfallen, as if she's about to cry. 'There was never such a thing as apartheid,' continues Elizabeth, jollily. 'We looked after our blacks well.'

———

Elizabeth is dumb, of course, but she is also very, very weird. Elizabeth thinks that the CIA are beaming sound waves through satellites to brainwash us. She thinks that her dog Tikka was proselytized by a secret One World Government to spy on her, and report its doggy findings back to Winnie Mandela.

'It took me years,' she says, 'to get old Tikka, my old doggy back.'

'It's terrible,' she says, 'when you can't even trust your own doggy.'

And she gazes out of the plane window, deep in thought, down at the mountains and the billows of black smoke where the Morula View Casino Complex was operating until today.

Things are getting too weird with Elizabeth, so I opt to bury my head in the in-flight magazine's travel supplement and make fascinated 'ooh' type noises at creatively spaced out intervals.

Astonishingly, there's an advert here for a 'Left-Handers Package Holiday', where left-handed people can sit on the beach and happily indulge in left-handed activities, far away from the heinous tyranny of our right-handed society. The slogan on the ad reads: 'Sick of patronizing resorts that don't cater for your left-handed requirements? Then visit Majorca's first left-hander-friendly self-catering holiday village'. I entertain the possibility of contacting the travel company with my suggestion for a more zappy axiom: 'Book Now! It's Statistically Proven We Die Younger!' but decide against it. They have a tough enough time as it is, what with all the right-handed corkscrews about.

Left-handers holidays, 'Womb-returning holidays' (something I read about in the *Independent on Sunday,* and not particularly high on my agenda either. My mother's womb resides in Merthyr Tydfil, and it takes a damn lot of encouragement to convince me to visit her house, let alone her internal organs), 'Murder-mystery weekends', 'White water rafting in Ecuador' and on and on. Christ, no. Sun City is just fine for me, war or no war. Sun City will be just fine.

We're five minutes away from the complex now, getting a little nervous. I'd been calling the hotel all morning from

Johannesburg, trying to confirm my booking. The woman was being as helpful as she could, which wasn't very helpful. You had to feel for her: all around the staff were chanting and screaming, baying for Mangope's blood. You could hear the screaming down the receiver.

'So is it a double room?' I asked. 'Do you have cable?'

'Call me back in two hours,' she yelled, and slammed down the phone.

So I lay back on the bed, switched on the TV, watched *It's Your Vote*, a touching daytime game show where contestants have to answer questions about electoral policy to win household appliances. Questions like: 'What do you do with a "ballot"?' It didn't matter whether they got the questions right or not. No: the studio audience had to vote on which contestant they liked the most. And the most affable and charismatic hopeful got to win the Hoover.

'What's our slogan?' the host grinned. The contestants yelled back, to cheesy organ music: 'We Must Accept The Election Result!'

'That's absolutely right,' sang the host, cheerfully. 'We certainly *must*!'

I switched over: another voter-education film. This time, a grandfather was telling his granddaughter about the bad old days before Mandela's release. About the blood of his people. About how they'd hang you if you slept with a white girl. And so on. The grandfather started to cry. Then he pulled himself together and said: 'But it's all different now. Now we can vote. Now, the future is *ours*. And I'm going to the polling station right now to practise how to vote.'

So – the film continued – he got all dressed up in his best suit, sauntered down to the polling station, head held high, practised filling in his ballot, pushed it into the box, and went home. Then we cut to the next day, and a surprisingly poignant twist in the plot: 'Grandad went to bed happy that night,' said the child. 'But he didn't snore like he usually does. That's because he was dead.' She paused, and continued, cheerfully: 'But at least he got to practise how to vote before he died.'

The film ended. I flicked off the TV, tuned the radio into one of their travel shows. 'Great Britain have just announced a tourist revenue of £19,000,000 for last year,' said the presenter. 'What wouldn't *we* do with £19,000,000?'

'Makes you want to cry,' agreed the co-host. 'Come on South Africans, let's pull our fingers out.'

And they did. Sun City phoned back, said I was welcome, but they were taking no responsibility for dead guests. And then I was on the plane.

————

We land into much yelling. The guests are being evacuated, shocked Germans not knowing what the hell's going on, being herded into 'Emergency Planes'. The bottle shop at Sun Village – a shopping complex outside the gates – is being looted, but they are leaving the other shops alone. This is targeted, ethical looting. The bottle shop was owned by Mangope's son.

At the gate, rumours are spreading that Mangope *had* been there, and was, at any moment, to be smuggled out on a stretcher. The mood is evil, locals and staff members and ANC supporters from around the region screaming and demanding revenge for a decade of tyranny. There's no talking to these people. Today is not a good day to be stretcher-bound in Sun City.

My Englishness takes over, my Englishness pushes the words out of my mouth in the middle of all this mayhem, the screaming and rioting and shooting. Amongst all this, I hear myself announce, 'Ahem. Excuse me. I have a reservation. The name's Ronson.'

'Get onto the fucking plane,' shouts a man with a gun.

And I get back onto the plane.

————

2

I wake up the next morning from a stuffy, disgusting sleep. Johannesburg is screaming with noise: traffic, the yells of the crowd. When I wake, I know exactly what I have to do. I have to get back to Sun City. The mood was calmer in Bophuthatswana today, the newspaper said. An uneasy calm. I look out the window at the dirty, hot streets, the uneasy calm of Johannesburg, an uneasy calm minus the waterfalls and casinos and authentic Africans dressed in authentic head gear. I think to myself: if I *have* to spend the day in an uneasy calm situation, I may as well do it sliding down a water-chute waving my arms in the air.

I call up Greg, my armed and helpful pal who has been provided as a complimentary service by the Johannesburg hotel to escort me places and sort out my travelling arrangements and shoot aggressors. I call him up and say, 'Greg. We've got to go back to Sun City. It is very urgent for us to do this.'

'Meet me in the lobby in five minutes,' he replies quickly. 'I will drive you there.'

So I head downstairs and meet Greg underneath the hotel's somewhat forbidding embroidered company motto hung up on the wall, 'For The Privileged Few'.

'Okay,' says Greg. 'Let's drive to Sun City. But first, there's something I want to do for you.'

'What?' I reply.

'There's something I haven't told you about my life.' He pauses, shyly. 'I run tourist bus tours of Soweto. And I want to take you on one. Just for you.'

'Really?' I reply. 'Bus tours of Soweto?'

'Yes,' says Greg. And he laughs and adds, 'For the privileged few to take photographs of the unprivileged many.'

———

Let me tell you a bit about Greg. Greg – like the grandfather in the film, the grandfather in his best suit – is convinced that, come the election, everything is going to be wonderful and

———

fabulous and rich and equal and nobody will kill anybody ever again.

Unlike the grandfather, however, Greg refuses to lament about the past.

'Ach, forgive and forget,' he says. 'We must look to the future. Mandela himself said that.' And he pauses, and adds: 'Oh! If Mandela ever dies, he'll be sitting up there right next to God.'

The first time I met Greg – the day before yesterday – was when he was showing me up to my room. Of course, I was thrilled to have an armed and eager-to-please pal to take me around – it's every man's dream. 'I'll do *anything*,' he said. 'Just ask. *Anything*.' And Greg certainly was helpful. Once inside the room, he pointed out the bed, the bathroom, the television, the mini-bar, the mini-bar key, how to open the mini-bar, and then he said, 'As you can see, the mini-bar stocks a large range of drinks.'

'Thanks, Greg,' I replied.

'Coke, whiskey, juice,' continued Greg, happily.

'Well, thanks Greg.' And I yawned and stretched my arms flamboyantly.

'Peanuts,' said Greg. 'Brandy, chocolates . . .'

'Yeah yeah okay, Greg. Look, I *just need* to be *left alone now*,' I snapped. And there you go. I'd been in South Africa for just a few days and I was already behaving incredibly boorishly to a township dweller whose job it is to leave home at 4.30 a.m., drive into opulent Johannesburg, and work for twelve, fifteen hours a day providing comfort for the wealthy whites for a fraction of the salary that his English counterpart would earn. White supremacy does the strangest things to you.

But Greg didn't seem to mind. 'Vodka,' he said. 'And, look. A bottle opener.'

———

And now we're driving to Soweto, right on the outskirts of Johannesburg, a twenty-minute drive past Chinatown, past the big sign that reads: 'YOU ARE ENTERING ARMED

———

RESPONSE COUNTRY', a turn off the freeway, round the corner, and straight into a huge mound of rubbish.

'Sorry,' says Greg, backing out of the huge mound of rubbish. 'My mind was elsewhere.'

Then we carry on down the road for a while, past a sign that announces, 'Welcome To Soweto', the two of us in a clapped out old BMW, bouncing up and down on the increasingly unkempt roads.

It's right after we pass the sign that Greg turns weird.

'Well, hello ladies and gentlemen,' he suddenly announces, 'and welcome to Soweto.'

'Greg?' I say, smally. 'What are you doing?'

'I suppose you're all wondering what Soweto means,' he continues, obstreperously, to the whole car.

'Greg you're scaring me,' I reply.

'It means South Western Township,' says Greg. And so on.

———

'If you turn to your right,' says Greg (I turn to my right), 'you will see our Kentucky Fried Chicken. But this isn't the only restaurant we have in Soweto. Oh no. We have a Chicken Lickin' as well. Which we'll be passing later on in the tour . . .'

The morning progresses in this fashion. We drive through endless shantytowns where emaciated, ragged children play in the dirt around festering open sewers and intimidating piles of discarded rubbish. Shantytowns have sprung up wherever there was free land – and they are a ramshackle collection of tarpaulin and brick, polythene and fetid stone. Greg asks me what I think about that, and I say, 'Tssk, terrible.'

Then we drive through some of Soweto's more opulent districts. When Greg told me that the township housed a smattering of affluent neighbourhoods, I thought he was being ironic, so I laughed sardonically. But a turn around the corner from the decay of the shantytowns – maybe thirty yards away – and you find yourself in a district that resembles the suburbs of Bournemouth. The father washes his expensive car in the driveway, the well-fed children play in the garden with their skipping ropes. Greg asks me what I think about that, and I say, 'Well, you'd never have thought.'

I get out of the car in an attempt to chat to the children, but they stare at me blankly, diffidently. This is not unusual: many children stare at adults with bellicose expressions. But there is something unnerving about these children, about the way they bristle. There is an expression in their faces that a child that young shouldn't have. And then I realize what it is. These children have learnt how to hate – in much the same way that the fathers, who grin and wave and offer me corn-on-the-cob, have learnt how not to.

Anyway, the tour turns out to be fun. We go to Nelson Mandela's old 'matchbox' house – very small – just like the countless other 'matchbox' houses in Soweto, except Mandela's is surrounded by high walls and trees to dissuade prying eyes. Then we go to Winnie Mandela's new house.

'It has sixteen rooms,' says Greg. '*Sixteen*! Can you imagine that? Are there any questions?'

I put up my hand. 'Greg,' I say, 'What has happened to Winnie Mandela's football team?'

'Ah,' he replies. 'You are referring to the famous private army that Maa Mandela employed for her safety.'

'Yes,' I reply.

'It has been disbanded since the problems.'

'You mean when she'd use them to beat her opponents to a bloodied pulp?'

'Well,' replies Greg, slowly. 'You must understand that her beloved husband had been in jail for many years, and when a woman is without her husband, she gets very upset and lonely. Shall we move on now?'

And we do. I'm eyed suspiciously by some, until they realize that I can't be AWB because I'm not very fat and don't have a very big beard. Then they surround me and spend the next twenty minutes eagerly persuading me of their ill-documented moral fibre. Which is lucky, really. Nothing – not a thousand viewings of *Cry Freedom*, not a million choruses of 'I Shall Be Released' – will prepare you for the shock of being besieged by thirty gaunt township dwellers all shouting at once.

I behave appallingly. I overcompensate. I clutch my wallet. I protect my wellbeing by attempting to imbue it with a grave political significance, a deceptively tricky feat that I am proud of to this day.

'We are a kind and honest people,' says one. 'We will not stab you or rape your wife.'

'That's *good*,' I reply, nodding thoughtfully. 'That's *very important* for the future of your country.'

'Mandela himself said we should love the white man,' says another.

'Mandela was absolutely right,' I reply, warming to my theme. 'Your infrastructure is dependent on it.'

'If we stabbed you now,' continues the first, 'then the media would turn against us.'

'They certainly would,' I reply. 'And you know how powerful the media is in influencing popular opinion.'

Then the conversation turns to the Bophuthatswana uprising, and the AWB's weird presence in the area. Terre' Blanche was now claiming that Mangope had invited him in there, which was kind of difficult to believe. 'An old man needed us, so we came,' he'd just announced in a press conference, and you could hear the journalists' sniggers. It's hard to take a man seriously who – every time he opens his mouth – sounds like he's making a speech from *The Hobbit*. But here in Soweto, people were taking his presence very seriously.

'What were the whites doing there?' yells one youngster. 'What were *you* doing there?' He comes up very close to my face and runs suddenly backwards, as if his anger is controlling his body.

'I had a reservation at Sun City,' I whine, and glance at Greg, who is already toying with his pistol. He shakes his head wearily at my response. And then we get back into the car, and end the tour.

'Thank you very much for choosing me as your driver,' says Greg. 'I hope that we had a very good time together and that it was an afternoon that you'll never forget.'

I clap, slightly embarrassed, and ask him how his enterprise is going. Not so well, is his reply, but there's hope. He's planning offshoots – overpriced Soweto souvenirs for the wealthy tourists. He's already patented a Winnie Mandela jigsaw, and is planning further jigsaws of Joe Slovo, Nelson Mandela and a Chris Hani memorial jigsaw.

I consider explaining that the 'Winnie-saw' may not be such a great idea. Since she initiated her tireless – some would say party-pooping – campaign to ban beauty contests and topless go-go dancing from the new South Africa, her position as Tourists' Favourite has taken something of a nosedive. But Greg considers Maa Mandela to be nothing short of a goddess, so I decide not to take the matter any further.

Later, we stop by at a hardware market where a lady offers to sell me a tea-towel that reads: 'EVERYTHING I HAVE YOU CAN SHARE, EXCEPT MY HUSBAND.'

––––

I want something to read for the journey to Sun City, so we head to Soweto's newsstand, which is a bunch of yellowing ragged magazines lying in a row on the pavement. It is an odd cluster. Old copies of *Hello*! magazine from 1989 – ' Ferdinand Marcos At Home With His Wife's Delightful Footwear' – nestle next to a seemingly arbitrary collection of specialist magazines, *Shoe and Leather News, Rubber and Plastics Weekly,* and so on.

There are very few porno mags: pornography is so heavily regulated here that some make do with *National Geographic*-esque picture-postcards of overweight topless Zulu women hurtling towards the camera clutching spears – hardly the most sparkling erotic reverie, unless you're a particularly weird Freudian. I opt eventually for a copy of *Femina*, South Africa's version of *Cosmopolitan*. Most of it is pretty staple fare: a feature on 'Gynacologists Who Abuse Their Patients' lies next to an in-depth interview with a South African ex-Miss Universe who – these days – is bravely battling bowel cancer in the privacy of her elegant Cape Town home.

'The last thing I wanted to do when I discovered my terrible illness,' she tells the magazine, 'was use it for publicity purposes. This is a private disease, and I don't want to exploit it to further my career.'

To illustrate the article there's a photograph of her in her hospital bed looking radiant and fastidiously made-up, and

––––

grinning courageously. Poor lady: she must have been furious when she discovered that what she thought was a cosy intimate chat and photo session was secretly published in a high-profile, high-circulation glossy monthly and distributed throughout the land.

I close the magazine and gaze out the window. I'm on my way to Sun City – down the freeway, past the sunflowers and tiny blue and purple flowers, and along the road where, every twenty yards, a placard reads 'Sun City – The Road To Riches'.

The closer we get to Bophuthatswana, trucks and tanks and other armoured vehicles crash past us, sending us careering into the hard shoulder. This route – the only road from Johannesburg to Mangope's homeland – is, basically, a one-lane motorway, and the entire South African Defence Force appears to be right behind us, honking angrily as they struggle to get past. It is infuriating. There is nothing more appalling to me than having a monstrous vehicle hurtle past with the force of an explosion, blaring its horn, spitting stones into the windscreen.

Back in England, I've long argued that lorries should be banned altogether from the motorways (and made instead to drive through the crumbling streets of our historic country villages), and, as far as I'm concerned, the same goes for South Africa. In England, I have a foolproof revenge tactic of frantically waving and pointing at their tyres while mouthing the words 'Puncture! Puncture!' the minute they try to overtake. But, under the circumstances, what with the SADF's emergency powers and all, I choose not to adopt it here. You know what states of emergency are like: a song and a smile here, an electrode implanted in your scrotum there.

We pull up at Sun City's entrance gate finally. The complex has closed for the war, and armed guards are patrolling the area, turning away guests and rioters and media people.

I say, 'I've got a reservation.'

'Please go away now,' replies the guard.

'I'm a *journalist*,' I continue, stupidly. 'The public has a right to know.'

'No journalists,' says the guard.

'What's going on inside that reporters aren't allowed to see?' I ask, in a guileful endeavour to weed out the truth.

'Look,' says the guard. 'You must leave now.'

'You're censoring the facts,' I yell.

'Oh piss off,' says the guard.

And so on.

———

So Greg and I head down to Sun Village and hang around the shops, sniffing a scoop. What are they hiding? What terrible secret deeds are taking place inside the complex that we aren't allowed to witness? And anyway, I have a reservation. I'm not going to allow some jobsworth with an AK47 to interfere with my inalienable right as a tourist to sit by a fake waterfall reading a good Sidney Sheldon book. That's all I want to do.

Then the man at the garage tells me the most upsetting thing of all: that there *are* guests in Sun City, that those holidaymakers who can't get back to their homes have been permitted to stay. The entire Australian cricket team are inside, I'm told, and I get excited. An odd reaction, really: I wouldn't recognize the Australian cricket team even if they ran towards me clutching wickets and yelling 'Six!'. But it's the thought of it. Outside the gates it's dusty and barren and the sun beats down, piercing a hole in your skin. The sun beats down inside Sun City too, but it's doesn't puncture you: it bathes you.

The casinos are open. The pools are working. Okay: the locals are up in arms against Mangope's alleged visit to the hotel, against Mangope's well-documented curious friendship with Sol Kersner – the dictator and the hotelier – so there's nobody there willing to call me 'master', but, fuck it, I can handle that. And God is smiling down on me today, for just as I wonder how the hell I'm going to get inside the complex, a young blonde man on a motorbike pulls up, a hairdresser from one of the salons.

'Are you okay?' he says. (I shall call him Simon: I've been informed that Sol Kersner deals with unruly staff in a similar vein to the way Lyle Menendez deals with unruly fathers, and the last thing I want to do is get Simon into trouble.)

———

'I'm trying to get inside.'

'You're not a journalist?' says Simon.

'Well, um,' I reply.

'Oh jump on,' he says.

I look over to Greg, who nods happily, motions that he will wait for me, indicates that it is absolutely fine to leave him here in the boiling heat for as long as I want, while I go off and sun myself. Greg gives me the thumbs up, gives me a 'don't y'all worry about me, just go and have yourself a good ol' time' expression, so I do.

Simon revs up the engine, drives me up through the mountains, through the staff gates, dumps me by the pool, drives off. And there I am, slap bang in the middle of an eerie emptiness, a ghost town. The hotel's ANC-supporting employees have cut down all the flags, and terrified the guests by dancing a scary tribal protest dance (subtly but tellingly different from their usual, nightly, scary tribal fun dance in that they didn't grin and bow afterwards), but now they've gone home too. I call room service and nobody answers.

So, this is what the dual powers of Sun International and the South African Defence Force are so anxiously safeguarding here in the Bophuthatswana mountains: a nothingness. A pleasure dome where there's no pleasure to be had. On any other day, Sun City would be alive with naked, gyrating dancing girls, prostitutes, Bryan Adams concerts, 'Win Your Dream Car' and 'Miss World' competitions, and on and on.

You have to respect them for that – it's not often you can create so much fun slap bang in the middle of a dictatorship. A funny thing about the Afrikaners: amidst all the mayhem and civil wars and necklacing and everybody stabbing each other in the head, they still know how to have a party. Admittedly, their parties are let down by the irksome fact that they are monumentally dumb. This is the one race of people with the admirable fortitude to set up a fancy Japanese restaurant in the middle of a war zone, and then go and blow it by calling it 'Origami'. This is the one race of people who – right in the middle of a potentially cataclysmic civil unrest – will *still* broadcast game shows where the announcer says, 'And our next victim . . . I mean, huh huh! *guest* is . . .'

And indeed, the croupiers are still here, standing forlornly by the empty blackjack tables. In a casino the size of a football stadium, only two people are gambling: Nigel, a loud and flash and tough management supervisor from Cape Town, who wears a baseball cap because he's just beginning to go bald, and his friend Spike, a huge Afrikaner in an open-neck shirt.

'I told them that I wasn't fucking going,' says Nigel, throwing down money and plastic onto the roulette table. 'I've come all the way from Cape Town, and I'm not going to fucking go home *now*. Are you a Jew?'

'Yes,' I reply.

'I know a Jew who married a Nazi. What do you think about that?'

'Well,' I mumble. 'If they're happy . . .'

'Of course they're not fucking happy,' he snaps. 'She's a Jew. He's a Nazi. How can they ever be *happy*?'

'So, um, why did they . . .'

'I've been asking them that question for years. Who knows. Fucking the enemy. Who knows.'

We settle into a slightly embarrassed silence, so – habitually – I ask him his views on the election.

'Ach,' he replies. 'Free elections are the most wonderful thing that ever happened to this country.'

'Really?' I say, surprised.

'Oh yes,' he replies, throwing $50 onto number ten. We are silent while the ball flitters across the wheel, lands next door. He shrugs, and continues.

'Yes, you need to give the Kaffirs their self-respect. They've been oppressed for too long. You know, my father used to whip them with a rhino hide when they didn't cut enough cane plants. He'd tie them up and give them a good hiding. He gave *me* a hiding once when I shot a horse for fun, and I'll tell you, that rhino hide hurts. But South Africa can't go on like that. We need to change with the times.'

'I'm pleased to hear you say that,' I reply.

'You know,' he continues blankly, 'I'm going to drive my blacks down to the polling station *myself*, I'm so in favour of the election.' He pauses for a moment, and adds, 'As long as they don't vote for the ANC.'

There's a silence. And then, Nigel says, slowly and wisely, 'It's not only the blacks you can't trust, just look at Spike. Spike is an Afrikaner – a Dutchman – and he's not educated. He speaks without thinking. He's a pain in the fucking arse. He can *never* make a decision.'

We glance over at Spike, playing the fruit machine in the corner. He looks back and waves happily. We grin, and Nigel moves over to the blackjack.

A moment later, Spike sidles up to me and whispers, 'Let me tell you something about Nigel. He's a brilliant man. *Brilliant*. He's a genius, is Nigel. A *millionaire*.' And he whistles, shakes his head in awe.

'And I'll tell you something *else*,' he continues briskly. 'Things were *good* before this election business. We had no problem: no gays, and no *lewdness*. But look at it *now*.'

He's right. I've only been in South Africa for two days, and I can testify for sure: lewdness is everywhere. Barely an hour after I arrived in Johannesburg, I was handed a leaflet inviting me to the opening of a non-pornographic photography exhibition of women's vulvas at a left-wing arts centre in the middle of town. Unfortunately, I'd only just got off the plane and, in my jet-lagged haze, I thought that the woman was talking about a non-pornographic exhibition of photographs of women's Volvos. Consequently, a muddled conversation ensued where she had to spend twenty minutes convincing me that – in her country – Volvos *were* sometimes considered pornographic, and that it was vital to explode that particular myth.

'Volvos aren't just there to be lusted after by men,' I heard her say.

'I personally have never found them attractive,' I replied. 'Ah, human sexuality is such a mystery to me.'

'Well,' she said, 'you surprise me. Most men do.'

It was only later that I pondered upon the conversation, deciphered the confusion, and kicked myself for passing up such an opportunity. One man's dogmatic inculpation of sexual bigotry is another man's opportunity to point and giggle. And that man would have been me. Spike goes silent

on me now, so I head outside and sit by the pool and fall
asleep for a bit.

———

By now, Eugene Terre'Blanche has pulled his troops out of
Bophuthatswana, and the war is all but finished. (The papers
were, to my chagrin, beginning to describe the events as a
'skirmish'. But I come from Cardiff, and, in my definition,
anything involving carnage and extensive billows of black
smoke is most certainly a war. In Cardiff, a 'skirmish' is what
happens when somebody gets slapped during a quarrel. I'll be
damned if I'm going to go back home and tell my friends that
I was in a *skirmish*. What does *that* mean?)

But *my* war is not yet over. I am woken by the sound of
a large barking dog. I blink, and see two young black men
patrolling the patio, looking dutifully around them, glancing
behind trees – the lot. They can't be older than seventeen.
The dog howls, and, when it sees me, it lurches out of the
boys' hands and starts charging frantically in my direction.
Quick as a flash, one of the youngsters jumps into the air,
lands on the dog, and sends it careering into the swimming
pool.

They grin, and shrug an apology, as the dog paddles
sheepishly towards the shallow end.

'Are you looking for Mangope?' I ask them.

The boys shrug.

'Have you seen him?' says one.

'Sorry,' I reply. 'But if I do . . .'

'Don't worry,' interrupts the boy. And then he adds, with
little sign of irony, 'Enjoy your wonderful holiday.'

And they head towards the waterfalls, glancing osten-
tatiously around them, practically checking underneath large
rocks for signs of the potentially cowering dictator.

———

As I sit here by the pool, I plan my next move. I have heard
that the big game hunting season has just begun in Zimbabwe,
so I make a spur of the moment decision to fly to Victoria
Falls and try and get in on a hunt. To foster my enthusiasm,

———

I read the official Zimbabwe tourist brochure that I'd collected from the Johannesburg tourist office. 'Zimbabwe' it begins, 'A Beautiful Country With A Sound Infrastructure.'

What a comforting slogan, I think. How calming. 'Victoria Falls is home to the lavish, glittering Victoria Falls Hotel, one of the greatest hotels in the World,' the brochure continues. 'The hotel stands next to the fabulously wet and flowing Waterfalls, which' – I'm paraphrasing here – 'are like gazing into a tremendous amount of water flowing a lot, but somehow more transcendental.' Once you've experienced Victoria Falls, by all accounts, you can hold your head up and announce, 'Now I've seen water.' The Jungle Tours overland safari fun holiday is leaving from Harare in a week too, so if the hunt doesn't work out, there's always that to fall back on. So, farewell, Bophuthatswana, my volatile friend, farewell. Things can only get better.

3

And, indeed, they do. The flight from Johannesburg was fine and comfortable – I'd convinced Air Zimbabwe to upgrade me to first class by saying, 'I've been in a war and I need a good sleep,' and they replied, 'You were in Bophuthatswana? It must've been terrible,' and I gave them a complex and mysterious 'War Changes You' look, like Robert Duvall in *Apocalypse Now*, although Robert Duvall had something of an advantage of not wearing comedy bermuda shorts and an unpleasant straw hat when he announced that the smell of napalm in the morning smelt like victory. The only war I looked like I'd been in that day was War 18–30. Remarkably, however, the ruse worked, and they upgraded me.

As part of the first class service, they summoned a young black man to carry my four enormously heavy bags through the airport, and he bowed and called me 'boss' in the boiling heat. I asked him how he was going to vote, and he thought for a moment.

'I like the Afrikaner,' he replied, eventually. 'He calls me "Kaffir", he orders me about, but he gives me the biggest tips.'

He laughed. I mentioned to him the poll that has just been published in the South African *Sunday Times*, which revealed the extraordinary findings that forty-five per cent of blacks questioned 'would rather be governed by an Afrikaner' than the named alternatives: a white, ANC-supporting liberal, or even a black businessman. He nodded sagely. I asked him who treated him the worst under apartheid, and his reply was swift.

'The English.'

'You mean the old colonial settlers?' I asked.

'Oh no,' he replied. 'They were good to me. No no. I mean the English tourists.'

———

Air Zimbabwe have an odd habit when it comes to their first class passengers: they make you sign a visitors' book before the plane actually takes off. I was in a quandary. I wanted to

———

write something nice – they'd been kind to upgrade me, after all – but all that had occurred so far was that I had sat down. I toyed with the phrase 'Excellent sitting down', but felt that it appeared half-hearted. Somebody up the page had written 'Exquisite fish', and this made me jealous. What were they doing handing out complimentary fish to some boarding passengers and not others? South Africa, I thought, sagely, a country of such stark inequality.

'Curious,' I said out loud, contemplated the page for a moment, and scribbled down 'Upholstery unbeatable'.

I landed in Harare early in the morning, and slipped through customs without a hitch (a surprise at first – it had been a long few days and I was grubby and dishevelled – but then I remembered the unfathomable logic enjoyed by customs officers worldwide, the more you resemble, say, Jethro Tull, the more likely they are to bustle you through with a wave and a grin, before strip-searching the fourteen-year-old Mormon boy in a bow-tie who's queueing up behind you).

I had time to kill before the connecting flight, so I spent the day walking the streets. Harare appears to have ground to an aesthetic halt somewhere around 1975, when Woolworth's and What Every Girl Wants were in their heyday and suedette was considered snazzy. The shops and offices all have that creepy built-to-collapse design that you'd find in a comprehensive school situated on the outskirts of Cardiff. Their infrastructure may be secure, but their buildings certainly aren't.

The stores sell a bizarre jumble of goods which, invariably, are altogether unconnected to what you'd expect from the name above the door. Thus, the 'UNISEX CLOTHING COMPANY – WHERE ALL THE FASHIONABLE PEOPLE GO' has a frozen food counter that sells carriage clocks and a stationery department which is big on corned beef. I bought my suntan lotion from a fish shop ($35 Zim – about £3.10). This was somewhat illegal, I subsequently learnt from the man at the press office. Foreign visitors are heartily discouraged from spending Zim currency. (So are, by the way, Zim residents. A rape case in a village outside Harare was settled – the day I arrived – by the rapist in question being fined three goats, a sheep, and a female member of his family to be donated to one of the victim's cousins. What a depressing country it must be when your odd aunt Agnes is harder currency than something you get from a bank.)

———

I spent the next three hours attempting to win myself a press card with which to impress the big game hunters in Victoria Falls. Of course, the bureaucracy in Zimbabwe is as unpleasant as it is in any country where one is obliged by law to refer to the president as 'Comrade' instead of 'that philandering crook'. I'd been told by the man at customs that the Ministry of Information had a press card authorization room, and discovering its whereabouts was the first hurdle.

'The Ministry of Information?' said the man selling the elegantly carved wooden giraffes. 'I've never heard of it.'

'Do you know who can direct me?' I asked.

'You should try the Information Ministry,' he replied. 'They may be able to tell you where it is.'

'Ah,' I said. 'How do I get there?'

'I don't know,' replied the man.

Finally, I tracked the place down. It was screaming with heat, the foyer packed with tense, perspiring visitors, queuing up to sign the admissions book. When it finally got to my turn, the doorman looked down at my entry and said, 'Show me your press card.'

'Ah,' I replied. 'I'm going to the press card authorization room now. That's why I'm here.'

'You can't go in without a press card,' he said, scratching his forehead.

'Are you telling me,' I said slowly, 'that I need a press card to allow me access to the press card authorization room?'

'That's correct,' said the doorman.

'Okay,' I said. 'Help me out here.'

'Get a press card,' he replied.

'From where?'

'The authorization room.'

'Upstairs?'

'Yes. Fifth floor.'

———

'Okay.'

I took a tentative step towards the lift, and turned quickly around. He was still staring, but made no effort to stop me. Things were looking good. I took another step.

'Wait,' he said abruptly. 'I cannot let you in without a press card.'

'For God's sake, man,' I yelled. 'What the hell can I do?'

'I don't know,' he shook his head sadly. 'I don't know.'

'Well, what do you do with other journalists?'

'I send them to the room that authorizes temporary one-day press cards,' he replied, lazily.

'Where's that?' I said.

'Upstairs,' he replied.

'And do I need a press card to get into that room?' I said.

'No.'

'Not even a one-day one?'

'No.'

'Can I go to that room now?'

'No.'

'Why not?'

'It's closed for lunch.'

'Ah ha,' I said. 'And when does it re-open?'

'In about five minutes.'

'Can I wait?'

The doorman looked behind me at the queue of fifteen sweaty people savagely tapping their feet on the floor and glaring at the two of us with ill-concealed loathing in their eyes.

'You have to wait outside,' he said.

I stormed out into the blazing heat, mumbling, 'fucking . . . Kafka . . . fucking . . . bring back Colonial rule . . . fucking . . .' I smoked a cigarette, turned swiftly around on my heels, and walked back in again.

'Where's your press card?' said the doorman.

'NOW JUST YOU . . .'

'I'm joking,' he said. 'Second floor.'

———

It was 3.00 p.m. when I caught my connecting flight to Victoria

———

36

Falls, Zimbabwe's home of the hunt. The first step was to try and get myself a complimentary room, so I headed straight to the Victoria Falls Hotel, which was, as the brochure suggested, a breathtaking old colonial building, charming and picturesque. Built against the rainforest between the steam railway track and the river, the hotel's views were astounding – spray erupting from the nearby waterfall, set alight by perpetually mutating rainbows.

I took off my straw hat, brushed down my hair, and headed, with a little anxiety, towards the public relations office. Of course, nobody likes to grovel in mud like a lowly worm, pleading with surly pen-pushers for scraps and leftovers, but, in these situations, I choose to comfort myself with the belief that a victory for me in the 'Free Room At Top Hotel' stakes is a triumph for Ronsons in general.

Throughout my childhood, you see, my family were constantly entering competitions. 'Win A Night At An Exclusive London Hotel'. That sort of thing. But victory unremittingly eluded us (aside from a bittersweet occasion when I triumphed in the 'Win A Fish' jamboree at the Cardiff High School fete. But it was a big con: the fucker was soiled, and didn't last the journey home.)

We tried and tried. We'd be constantly filling out forms, completing sentences in no more than twenty words. And our perpetual defeats were made all the more ironic by the fact that the previous owner of our house, a Mr Franklyn, was the luckiest man alive.

'Congratulations, Mr Franklyn,' proclaimed the letters that arrived daily. 'You have almost certainly won HALF A MILLION POUNDS.' 'Mr James Franklyn,' they continued, 'You have been chosen from all the people living in SOUTH CARDIFF to receive this FREE PERSONALIZED STATIONERY and probably an AUSTIN MONTEGO.'

It was tough all round. Poor James Franklyn, who had left no forwarding address, was wholly unaware of the disproportionate catalogue of glittering fortune being showered upon him, and we Ronsons were getting to the stage where we could not bear not being James Franklyn any longer.

It was never stated. My mother would simply pick up the

letters each morning, glance voicelessly at their contents, and place them mournfully in a pile on a table by the front door. Then every day, on our way to school, we would file gloomily past the mound – a growing and ironic testament to the fortunes of a non-Ronson, and wonder how long this could go on.

One morning, a tantalizing letter arrived informing the swine that if he successfully scratched off the three gold circles to reveal matching '$' signs, he would DEFINITELY receive a NIGHT AT THE RITZ. All he had to do – should he be serendipitous enough to win – was bring some identification to an office complex in town, watch a short film on the rhapsody of timeshare, and the prize was his.

We broke then. It was all too much. That day, our family made an wicked, covert pact. We would scratch away and be damned with the consequences. So we did, hearts a-fluttering. And *yes*! by God – *three*! We had won, Franklyn and us.

So, twenty minutes later, my father and I approached the office. 'We're the Franklyns,' he announced ebulliently, 'the lucky winners.'

'Ah, Mr Franklyn,' replied the receptionist, 'Congratulations. Have you bought any identification?'

'I certainly have,' replied my Dad, searching nonchalantly for his wallet before slapping his forehead with impeccably executed horror, 'Damn. I must have left it at home. Hang on. Will this personalized stationery do?'

'That's fine,' replied the receptionist. 'Just wait here.'

So we sat and waited, perturbed somewhat by the procession of additional lucky winners that were slowly filling the chairs. Exhilarated ageing couples plucked from across Cardiff, winking euphorically at each other, sharing the collective rapture of victory. And then, a pristine Nazi type in a pinstripe skirt started calling out our names, interrogating us, leading us into a back room.

'Mr and Mrs Wilson, Mr and Mrs York, Mr Franklyn. Mr Franklyn? James Franklyn?'

'Yes, yes, Franklyn here,' my Dad cried, the world's worst fraudster. My father is an upstanding man, and this, the one occasion in his life when he was forced into deceit, he fell completely to pieces.

'What's your line of work?' she asked.

'Oh um, this and that,' he replied. 'You know, things.'

'Are you married?'

'Yes.'

'Haven't you read the small print? You have to bring Mrs Franklyn along.'

'Bed-ridden,' I heard him explaining. 'She was bitten.'

'Oh. Well. Come this way.' And we stood and walked, with wide-eyed naiveté, into hell.

The short film about timeshare turned into an hour long video explaining – with coldly scientific accuracy and pie diagrams – that failure to spend a week every year in the same Majorca holiday complex would indubitably lead to financial ruin and being laughed out of fashionable society.

'What fool would choose a different holiday location every year?' scoffed the voice-over with chilling, compelling persuasiveness. And we scoffed along with glazed eyes and empty grins. I swear, had David Koresh been recruiting that afternoon, offering a surprise free gift for the first hundred converts, I would currently be one frazzled zealot.

Then, after coffee and digestives, the hard sell began. The pristine Nazi woman lunged towards us. 'Oh come on, Franklyn,' she said. 'Are you man or a mouse? Get out your credit card.'

'What?' my father replied, incredulously.

'What will your wife think when you tell her you turned *this* down?' she continued, almost spitting with disdain. 'She'll think you're an *idiot*.'

'What?'

'Just get out your credit card. Come on. Get it out.'

Forty-five minutes later, she gave up. We were empty husks, quaking, our will to live evaporated irrevocably. We quivered all the way to reception to collect our prize, a voucher for a night at Hotel Shite, Sunderland, the prerequisite being that we'd have to buy three meals a day there, at about £60 a head. But we had *won*, by heavens, and nobody was going to take that away from us, even if it meant spending the entire gala referring to each other as Franklyn. Which, indeed, we did.

It was, therefore, with a sense of apprehension that I approached the public relations department of the Victoria Falls Hotel. Imagine my delight, therefore, when it turned out that the PR officer was a charming and helpful lady, and offered me a room on the spot, the moment I showed her my press card.

'Goodness,' she said. 'You could do with a good sleep after what you must have gone through to get that.'

'It was hell,' I agreed, shaking my head sadly.

And when I got to the room, there was a bottle of wine and many different varieties of curious fruit waiting for me. I looked up to the ceiling, thanked God for bestowing His many magisterial gifts upon me, took a hot bath, sat down for a moment on the soft, comfortable bed and fell asleep for sixteen hours.

―――

I awoke in the morning, refreshed and eager to get myself onto the big game hunt. There was a newspaper pushed underneath my door, and I picked it up to discover that it was dated from this very day in 1902. What a delightful idea, I gurgled happily to myself. But my devotion towards the Vic Falls Hotel was so intense at that moment, that if there'd been a pamphlet pushed underneath my door saying 'Kill The Jews', I probably would have considered that delightful, too.

I took a long, leisurely breakfast, and planned my course of action. I had five days in which to succeed. The overland safari group, Jungle Tours, were leaving in a week, and it was just beginning to dawn on me what a potentially woeful blunder my inclusion on that trip could be. Over breakfast, I read their brochure more carefully now: the brochure that included the portentous phrases 'rising with the sun' and 'duties include gathering wood'. A worrying thought. Wood-gathering is not a strength of mine, not something I'm prac-tised in. The closest I've ever got to gathering wood is buying a box of matches from the local newsagents.

And then I thought: how will my fellow safari-goers cope

――――

with the knowledge that I am a deficient wood-gatherer? Will they turn against me, like the other boys turned against Piggy in *Lord Of The Flies*? Nobody likes a shabby wood-gatherer. Will they misinterpret it as a shortcoming of masculinity rather than an ideological antagonism towards wood-gatherers in general? Wood-gatherers and all they stand for.

For I believe this to be the case: today it's wood-gathering, hanging around in woodland, empathizing with tree-life, becoming disenfranchised with city-dwelling. Tomorrow it's liberating forests, lying in the way of bulldozers, anti-tarmac protests. And what if they win? In a tarmac-less society, we'd have nowhere to park our cars. Without cars, we'd have to walk everywhere, and we'd miss all our appointments. And without appointments – well – all we'd be left with is anarchy.

No: I am not a wood-gatherer, but neither am I a 'Don't Hug Me Too Hard – I'm Fragile' type of guy. I am a city boy: a product of the Industrial Revolution. I was convinced that when the pressure was on, my wood-gathering skills would transcend the word 'inadequate'. I knew that when my companions were depending on me to gather the *correct sort of wood* to make the fire, to ward off dangerous animals – combustible wood, wood that wasn't wet – I *knew* that I would end up bringing back pebbles.

I read further: the small print that stated (and this is the most extraordinary thing I have ever heard) 'all our African Safaris are based on camping. Sometimes this takes place in campsites, in the bush, in the garden of a friendly villager, or in the grounds of a hotel.' In the *grounds of a hotel*. How could I have missed *that*. What am I – a fucking wood pigeon? When I go to a hotel, I check in. I don't book into a Holiday Inn and sleep in the garden. And if the villagers are really that friendly, what's wrong with the spare room?

Then I read the 'Basic Kit' section, the section that included the suggestion that we bring along a multi-purpose knife. What was *that* about? Were we going to have to defend ourselves at any point? And a mosquito net. Did that mean that there might be *mosquitoes* there? The thought of combat with an insect was wholly alien to me. Okay: there may be much wisdom to be learnt from indigenous villagers, but at least, in Britain, the insects know who's boss. At least, in Britain, we've beaten the insects in the battle for supremacy.

And the tiny, tiny writing, the tiny wee writing that said that our 'duties' (the last time I performed a 'duty' was when I was twelve) included 'cleaning the vehicle'. I haven't cleaned a vehicle since they invented car-washes. I don't even know how to *spell* shammy leather. 'Sometimes in life you'll have to do things you don't want to,' my mother used to predict doomily when I was a child. And there you go, Gypsy Rose Ronson.

The Jungle Tours brochure went on to state that we must enter the experience with 'a positive outlook', that we must be prepared to 'pull our weight' or we will become 'very unpopular amongst the group'. And then the terrifying reality hit me with the force of an oncoming herd of rhinos: I was going to be in a *group*, and would, therefore, be obliged to sit by a campfire at night singing songs. A campfire fuelled by the wood which I had gathered.

Did the 'must' include joining in on 'If I Had A Hammer'? I don't know the words to 'I Am A Rock' or 'Ging Gang Gooley'. But fuck 'em and their positive attitude and their camp fire songs, I thought. Fuck 'em all, well in advance. I'm not a hippie: I'm a *journalist*.

I studied the brochure's typical 'group' photograph for clues of what *my* retinue would be like. There they were, all sitting atop a Land Rover, grinning, arms outstretched. One had hair extensions to make her look tribal, one was carrying a viola. They appeared elated: a bunch of blonde, muscled, Australian backpackers, the men standing by piles of wood, pointing at the wood, the women oozing respect for the quality of the heap.

And the onerous truth was staring at me from the photograph, from the expressions on the faces of the happy travellers: when you're in the jungle, wood counts. When you strip away all the materialism of bourgeois Western living, all the lies that can be purchased with hard currency – the cars, the flat, the nightclubs, when all that counts is the gathering of wood, the calibre and volume of the mound, then you'd better gather with vigour, for there will be no escape. Not even from yourself.

On the next page was a photo of a lion standing over a bloodied cadaver of an unfortunate wildebeest, who, one assumed, had spent too much time watching TV and going to restaurants to master the precarious ways of the jungle.

———

It was, therefore, with a renewed vigour and a firm resolve that I started making enquiries into getting a freebie on the hunt. I spent the next few days making telephone calls, sweet-talking dusty men with full beards. I settled into a routine, hanging around hunt centres in Victoria Falls Town during the day, lunching on a 'Livingstone Special' (tuna, anchovies, double cheese) in the 'I Presume Pizzeria', followed by supper in the Livingstone Restaurant before retiring to the 'I Presume' cocktail bar for after-dinner drinks.

What a pity, I thought, that the first white man to discover the Falls back in 1855 left behind such a small repertoire of quotable phrases with which to brighten the tourist industry that was to spring up in his wake. But things were made all the more irksome by the fact that Livingstone was also – it has now been recognized – a dog-faced old turd. He treated his wife and family like shit, and suffered a psychotic, often violent paranoia towards many of his friends, who, he was convinced, were constantly conspiring to screw up his life. But tourist industries being what tourist industries are, I guess that the 'Stop Staring At Me Or I'll Break Your Fucking Legs' cocktail bar doesn't have quite the same ring. ('Dr Livingstone, I presume.' 'No I'm not. Who told you? Fuck off.')

From the verandah of the hotel I spent the evenings gazing out at the seventy-year-old railway bridge built in the no-man's land between Zimbabwe and Zambia. It was on this bridge that Harold Wilson famously shook hands with Ian Smith and signed a historic declaration the jist of which nobody can quite remember, although they vigorously pretend to at all times. 'Ah,' they say, 'It was a unilateral treaty that was really terribly important to the wellbeing of many, many citizens.' Don't listen to these people. They are the same people who are adamant that the 1922 Committee is made up entirely of parliamentarians born in 1922, and that the Lloyd's Names are a large group of bankrupt people called Lloyd.

Nowadays the bridge is used solely for irritating pedants who've seen Victoria Falls from the Zimbabwe side to go see it from the Zambia side so they can tell people who didn't bother how much more breathtaking it was. That is the only reason to go to Zambia. Aside from the Falls, all Zambia has to offer is a vast amount of people staring angrily at you and trying to sell you elegantly carved wooden giraffes.

After making initial enquiries into the hunt, it began to dawn on me that it had to be a freebie or nothing. The hunt costs a fortune. Any decent trip (where you get to kill an elephant, two zebra, a crocodile and a couple of antelope) will set you back $35,000 US. And this is why: to get in on the hunt, you have to first go to an official hunting centre where you purchase your beasts. You actually buy them. Then you go out into the bush and shoot them.

Which begs the question, what happens if you miss? You still *own* the blighters. Do they present them to you at the airport? Do you have to take the fucking zebra home with you? Consequently I hoped – when push came to shove – I'd have a clear aim. I didn't want to be lumbered with a live zebra. Zebra are great for a while, with the stripes and all. But you get sick of them, and all you're left with then are crap horses that make good carpeting. (I shiver now to think of those days when I used to march with the anti-vivisectionists, through Kensington High Street, down into Philbeach Gardens, round some cul-de-sac or other, and back up into Kensington High Street: as if the organizers were attempting to structure a bizarre form of Zen protest, making us feel empathy with the laboratory rats by getting us to run round and round in circles all day. Thank God I am cured now of all that caring. Thank God that – nowadays – I can look at a zebra and all I see is a classy rug that's still walking.)

The next few days were kind of dull: hanging around, waiting for the phone to ring. I read the papers, saw a report in *The Herald*'s showbiz page that old Sol Kersner had put on a Natalie Cole gig at Sun City and invited all the ANC and Communist Party leaders along. They had a wonderful time, by all accounts. They danced up and down the aisles saying what an excellent place the Lost City was, and how they couldn't wait to bring their wives for a long weekend. (Ah, politics marches onwards.) And then, on the fourth night, just as I was wondering how long all this waiting could go on, the telephone rang.

4

So, downstairs, twenty minutes later, the big game hunter and the conservationist are having a clash – locking antlers on the patio – while eight Frenchmen, a South African liberal, me, and a flock of vicious, swooping beetles gaze on in startled silence.

'It's all down to chromosomes,' begins the hunter. 'The insect has no fucking chromosomes whatsoever. The big game have twenty chromosomes. The monkey has twenty-three, the black man has twenty-three-and-a-half, the Dutchman has twenty-three-and-three-quarters, and the white man has twenty-four chromosomes.'

He pauses, puts his arm around me, and adds, 'I'm a pragmatic man. Me and Jon. We're pragmatic men. We're *engineers*. We're not *romantics* like you are.'

I nod.

'So what does *that* prove?' says the conservationist. 'Just because the big game are dumb and look good, doesn't mean some prick with a gun should shoot them.'

'Don't you understand,' retorts Gary, the liberal. 'We need to shoot them so we can *conserve* them.'

'Look at the moths,' says the hunter sagely. 'Look at the moths in Jon's soup.'

The twelve of us turn and gaze at my French onion soup. It is manifestly saturated with the broken, lifeless bodies of many, many moths and one repulsive beetle struggling to clamber onto the floating cheese island. It is a hideous sight. If this were England, there'd be an outcry at insects so patently loathsome. If this were England, we'd have invented something luminous and deadly and plug-in before you could proclaim, 'That's no beetle – that's winged evil.'

But this is southern Africa, where the insects are frighteningly close to winning the battle for supremacy, buzzing around like they own the place. A naysayer would suggest that the humans are outnumbered to the extent that dignified surrender is the only course of action. But southern Africa is a law unto itself, where the underdog can – and often does –

come up trumps against all the odds. Take the Battle for Blood River in 1838. Three thousand Zulus prestigiously annihilated, with no Boer casualties whatsoever – an astounding victory celebrated by a whopping commemorative water tower in Pretoria. If the whites can pull off such a conquest against so many armed savages, then – one hopes – a great bug pogrom may still be around the corner.

'Yeah,' says the conservationist. 'So?'

'It proves *everything*,' I reply. 'If the moths didn't *want* to die, they wouldn't be diving into the soup.'

'Steady on,' says Doug, the hunter. 'They don't WANT to die. But it's all down to chromosomes.'

'It's true,' I say. 'You wouldn't see a white man diving into soup.'

'What about the Dutch?' says Trevor the conservationist. 'My *mother* was Dutch.'

'I'm not suggesting that *all* Dutch are feeble-minded,' replies Doug. 'But try giving them a country to run.'

'Yeah,' I say, rising to my feet. 'Look at Holland. It's all fucking . . . it's all fucking . . . women in costume . . .'

'The Afrikaners have done more for South Africa than . . . fucking . . .' Trevor's bubbling now.

'Yeah,' says Doug. 'They've done so much for South Africa that they're giving it to the black man.'

'Come on now,' say the liberals.

'CLOGS AND CRACK DEALERS,' I yell. 'What kind of a country is *that*?'

There is a furious silence, which I use to appraise the situation. I'm doing great, but it's been a tough few hours. My folly had been opting to go undercover as a successful construction engineer based in Newport, Gwent. (I'd been told how much the hunters hated journalists, and I had to think on my feet.)

It was a potentially tragic blunder, in retrospect, but I don't blame myself. How was I to know that Doug had a very special interest in piping? How was I to know that he'd been dying to discuss his piping theories for years with a fellow piping enthusiast? In all my travels, I have picked up one solitary piping phrase, 'the underground stemming effect', and

I've never been so glad of it as I am tonight. All night long it's been 'underground stemming' this, 'underground stemming' that.

It's been a worrying time, and I'm certain that my companions were beginning to suspect something. For a start, little more than a casual glance at my Fairy Liquid hands would reveal to a trained eye that I'm not, essentially, a construction engineer type. Secondly, the fact that I've spent the entire night pummelling them with questions about the complexities of the hunt world (stopping just short of getting them to spell their surnames and tell me their ages) has surely put seeds of doubt in the most trusting of minds. I may as well have been wearing a trilby with a press card sticking out of the rim for all my undercover prowess tonight. I may as well have been screaming 'hold the front page' into a telephone.

Finally, thank God, the conversation has switched to genetics, and the ineptitude of the Dutch in governmental affairs, and I am in my element. I gaze up at the stars. They are big and bright – like the stars you get at the London Planetarium. In the distance a hippo bobs his head out of the Zambezi river, and vanishes again, just like the hippos do at the Barry Island funfair logflume ride. The sunset has been and gone, and, for a moment, the sky was as blood red as a Roger Dean poster. I know where I am with nature tonight, and I feel safe.

So after days of hanging around, I'm finally face to face with my potential hosts. The money's all gone and if I don't get accepted here, I'm on the Jungle Tours overland safari bus by the weekend – a prospect that's becoming more and more loathsome as the days go by. The Frenchmen and the liberals have to approve of me, so does Doug. Trevor the conservationist has turned up out of the blue to cause trouble with his moral tantrums, and he can fuck off on a two-week caravan holiday with the beetles for all that concerns my plans.

But first I have to get onto the hunt, convince them to let me tag along. Three days ago, I contacted Doug's agent, a brash man called Tony, and things were looking hopeful.

'Lions, crocodiles or antelope?' he asked during our first conversation.

'What?'

'Do you want to see lions, crocodiles or antelope?'

'*See* them?' I said. 'No, no. *Shoot* them.'

'Yes yes,' replied Tony wearily. 'Lions, crocodiles or antelope?'

'Oh,' I said. 'Um . . . crocodiles?'

'You'll be wanting Doug in that case,' he replied. 'I'll call you when I reach him.'

So, 12.30 a.m. tonight: the phone rang. 'Jon. I've tracked down Doug. He's at your hotel *now* drinking with the bloody Frenchmen. Get down there, but don't mention my name. I've got nothing to do with this, okay?'

'So is the hunt on?' I muttered, blearily.

'It's up to Doug. Thin guy, can't miss him, he's with eight bloody Frenchman and a Frenchwoman. Don't tell them you're a journalist. If he says no, *don't* phone me again.' And, swiftly, he hung up.

I climbed out of bed and fumbled around for my acceptable footwear (the security guard at the 'I Presume' bar is a stickler for congenial shoes, I have learnt, and I don't want to be caught out again. This – one can only assume – is cheap, spiteful revenge for his own embarrassing regulation attire. Security guards across Zimbabwe have the luckless curse of being forced to wear statutory bright – almost luminous – lime-green uniforms and a building site hard hat straight out of the Village People. Their buttons and batons are as shiny as pearls, and the overall effect is rather like being admonished by a character from *Fraggle Rock*). I'd been waiting days for this moment, had my construction engineer ruse all worked out. But I was dazed now, and the last thing I wanted to do was skulk around the patio listening for French accents. So it was with some reluctance that I headed downstairs and prowled the bars until I discovered my quarry.

I recognized them immediately. The Frenchmen looked French in the way that only Frenchmen can – grubby, toothless, gesticulating with vigour. So I joined them, chatted away casually, and eventually we got to denigrating the Dutch, which swung it. It is widely recognized that Frenchmen *hate* the Dutch, with their fresh faces and undesirable tulips, and it was a clever move. Twenty minutes later, they invite me to tag along on the bus for the next day's hunt. I'm not allowed to actually *kill* the beast (I'd have to pay for that), but I'm more than welcome to watch it die. And that'll do. The Frenchmen and Gary are here for the duration. Their hunt is to last twenty-one days. Tomorrow they're just going for crocs. On Friday, it'll be kudu, or impala. Some nights, they'll camp in the bush, other nights they'll come back to the hotel. I am lucky. Tomorrow is just a day trip, and they'll get me home in time for dinner.

_____

6.30 a.m., Thursday. The sun is rising, and we're sitting in a twelve-seater Land Rover heading towards a huge private farm thirty kilometres from Vic Falls. The talk is all war stories of previous croc encounters – legs being bitten clean off, and so on, the hunters chatting themselves into a frenzy of croc hostility.

'Do you remember poor old Janos the poler?' says Doug. 'Lost both arms and the whole right side of his body to a croc back in '86. I had to *beat it* with a stick to release what was left of him.'

'And the worst thing of all,' adds Gary the liberal, 'is that I was only paid $25 for the photographs. Twenty-five fucking dollars. Can you believe it?' And we tut and shake our heads.

And, yes, by the time the journey ends, I *hate* those crocs. By the time we reach the camp, I'm convinced that the swine have formed a clandestine international reptilian conspiracy, and are solely responsible for the imminent breakdown of probity and righteousness the world across. Until today, my views on crocodiles were pretty much ambivalent, even positive. They were okay, I guessed, but I didn't want one babysitting my daughter. But now – Christ – let's kill the bastards. I'm raring to go.

The farm is a huge expanse of savanna, waterfalls, lakes and rivers. Like all white-run farms in Zimbabwe, the owners are living in perpetual fear of having it taken off them and given to a 'deserving black farmer', as part of Robert Mugabe's policy of farmland redistribution. Unfortunately, 'deserving' has been redefined in Zimbabwe-talk as 'high-ranking

_____

politician' or 'close friend of Robert Mugabe'. Therefore, across the land, ranches are being handed over to some Minister of Typewriting Fluid or other who doesn't know a sickle from shinola. This hunt, Doug points out gloomily, may be the last on this ranch.

The Frenchmen have purchased some antelope, an elephant, and a couple of zebra, but today is croc day, so we set up camp, build a fire, and plan our strategy, which consists, as far as I can tell, of finding a crocodile, and shooting it from a distance. I am put on campfire duty, and – yes – I pull off the rather astounding achievement of bringing back damp twigs. It hasn't rained for weeks, and these must be the only moist boughs in the whole of Zimbabwe.

Luckily, Doug doesn't mind. In fact, he responds by rubbing my nose. He rubs away vigorously, slaps me on the back, and rubs some more. 'I hope some of your Jew luck rubs off on me,' he announces, jovially. 'That's what I need today. Some of your Jew luck.'

Well, that's a fine hullabaloo, I think, but I can't help blaming myself. I'm the one who let slip my theological origins. I'd tried my best not to, knowing how much these people hate the Jews – but you know what it's like when the pressure's on. Usually, few aspects of my personality manifest themselves in a manner that people would consider 'Jewish', but when I'm undercover and mingling with racists, I inexplicably find myself turning into the cast of *Fiddler On the Roof*. I hunch my shoulders, order chopped liver in restaurants. It takes a huge amount of self-restraint to stop myself from rubbing my hands together and cooking everyone gefilte fish: something that doesn't go down too well with Nazis. It's a terrible, incomprehensible facet of my personality and I hate it.

I like Doug though. He's an honest racist, most South Africans are. It is unnerving – at first – to witness a man being so candidly sincere about his bigotry. It's not something we're used to: we're far more mannerly and cordial about the whole messy business. (Still, we'd never let the swine run our country.) The shock of coming here for the first time is pretty much the same as if the British National Party started advertising Make

New Friends open days with free entertainment and RAC signs proclaiming 'Pit Bull Terrier Fight First Left'.

And so the morning progresses. We split up into small groups. I'm with Gary and Doug. As we wander towards the river, I get chatting to Gary about my trip to Soweto, and he eagerly cross-questions me on the subject for about half an hour. Which surprises me.

'Haven't you ever been there yourself?' I ask.

'Oh, no no,' he replies, shocked. 'You must realize that we know *nothing* about the blacks. We *never* mixed. I only heard about the death of Biko two years ago. I only heard about the Soweto massacre last year. We were in the dark. We knew *nothing*.'

Then he asks, nervously, 'Did you meet anyone from the ANC?'

'Yes,' I reply.

'Did they . . .' He stutters a little. 'Did they mention anything about home humiliation?'

And he tells me about home humiliation, about the rumours going around Johannesburg of secret ANC documents authorizing the raping of the rich, white wives, the seizing of property – redistributing white farmland to black politicians, public floggings of apartheid stalwarts, murder and bloodshed, and on and on and on. Gary heard these rumours from his mother, who heard it from an aunt. Gary's mother cried.

Then Gary says, 'It's not that the blacks even want black rule. You only have to look at Zimbabwe to see how fucked up *that* is.' And he comes up close – conspiratorially – sips from his beer, and continues, 'In Zimbabwe, they *all* want Ian Smith back as their leader. It's all in the genes, and they know it. The blacks understand that they haven't the genes to rule a country. And they're comfortable with that. In ten years time, the ANC will be pleading for a reinstatement of apartheid.'

And, to qualify his point, he recounts a joke that one of his black employees told him on this very subject. Two Kaffirs are standing in a huge long queue at the bank. They've been standing there for hours, and are fed up. So one says to the other, 'I'm so sick of all this queuing, all this bureaucracy, that I'm going to assassinate Mugabe and get Ian Smith reinstated.' And with his friend's blessing, he goes off with his gun, but returns minutes later. 'That was quick,' says his friend. 'I didn't bother,' replies the Kaffir. 'The queue was *enormous*.'

We laugh, but Doug suddenly says, 'Shhhhh.' We're standing on the top of a crevice, and, down below, a crocodile nestles on the bank of a river. We are in silence now. The crocodile is motionless: it could be dead, for all it's moving.

'They never move,' whispers Gary. 'They just . . .'

Doug hands the gun to Gary. He slowly raises it to his eye level, and takes a shallow, quick breath, like the gunman does in the movie *Targets* when he's blowing away cars on the freeway. And then: 'No,' says Doug, abruptly. 'It's too far.'

'I can get it,' replies Gary. He's concentrating hard, and his words are coming out pained.

'You'll just injure it,' continues Doug calmly. 'You won't kill it, and we'll never get down there in time to finish it off.'

'I can *get it*,' says Gary slowly, and he raises the gun again.

'Look,' says Doug. 'You'll either miss entirely, or you'll injure it. Either way, there's no point in trying. We'll never retrieve it. No. Look I . . . No. Don't.'

The shot rings out across the valley, and the crocodile arches its back so far that its head almost touches its tail. It's in the river now, vanished, and the river is turning red.

'Damn,' says Gary, 'I missed it.'

'What?'

'I missed it,' he continues. 'And now it's gone. Come on. Let's go. Let's find another one.'

'Don't be ridiculous,' says Doug. 'Look at the blood.'

'The crocodile *heard* the shot,' replies Gary testily, '*jumped* into the water, and injured itself on a rock on the way in.'

'What?' says Doug incredulously.

'The croc's *fine*,' says Gary, his voice raising slightly. 'It's just a scratch.'

We look down at the river: there is no sign of life, the blood is dispersing now, and pretty soon the water will be back to its normal colour.

'It was just a scratch,' says Gary, but his voice, as it rises in anger, becomes more and more accented. By now he is saying, 'Lik. It wus jeest a scretch. Hu*kay*?'

In Doug's inside pocket is the list of animals it's okay for the tourists to shoot during the next three weeks. Gary has been allocated just one crocodile. If he shoots another, it will be cold-blooded murder, and not fun any more. Gary's outburst, therefore, puts something of a dampener on the day. There is a fine line, in the big game hunting world, between a healthy antagonism towards large animals in general and out-and-out psychosis, and Gary has crossed that line.

5

Back at the Vic Falls Hotel, the mood is tense, unmanageable.

Doug says, 'Do you want me to go back and *get* that fucking crocodile because I *will*.'

Gary says, 'Why would I lie about something like that? You *saw* it swim away.'

Doug says, 'Well we'll see how far it swam when I go back and get its fucking *corpse*.'

Gary says, 'Yeah, you just do that.'

Now the security guard from the 'I Presume' hurries angrily across to the table jangling and glistening like an irate Christmas decoration.

'Will you *please* be quiet now?' he hollers. 'This is a QUIET bar.'

'Sorry,' says Doug, sheepishly.

'I'm sorry,' says Trevor.

The guard brusquely readjusts his hard hat, and saunters away, passing underneath the huge framed photograph of Robert Mugabe that stares soberly down onto us all. This is the same photograph of Mugabe that can be found in hotels and offices and restaurants across Zimbabwe: the stoic states-man sitting stoically behind his presidential desk. To his left, a telephone on which he makes his indispensable calls. Behind him, Zimbabwe's flag flying proudly, as it has done for the past fourteen years.

Unfortunately, the photographer's light has caught Muga-be's face in a slightly peculiar manner, which makes it look uncannily as if there's a roasted almond resting between his nose and his upper lip, as if Mugabe was eating roasted almonds the day of the photo session, and one got stuck. I'm not the only person to have noticed this lamentable trick of the light. Just about every old Rhodesian I've met still living in Zimbabwe has pointed the almond out to me.

'Look at old Almond Face,' they chuckle. 'You'd have thought that somebody would have told him he had an almond stuck on his lip!'

I point it out now to Trevor and Doug, in a valiant attempt

to diffuse the brawl blaring between them, but it is to little avail.

'If you're not going to let me shoot another croc, then I want my money back,' yells Trevor. 'I'm not going to pay for a croc that lived.'

'Listen here . . .' says Doug.

'Look at old Almond Face!' I say, and so on.

And the battle rages on in this manner. But let me take you away from the hotel now, far, far away, over the gardens, over the waterfalls, across many oceans, and many years, to 1877, and a sickly twenty-four-year-old English boy from Bishop's Stortford, writing in his diary: 'I contend that we are the finest race in the world, and the more of the world we inhabit the better it is for the human race.'

Anyway, they named a country after him. They wanted to call it Cecilia, but that name seemed too womanly for all the high hopes he had for it: a majestic land where the white man could build a paradise for himself, a paradise of gold and diamonds and a regal railway stretching from Cairo to the Cape, and invite other white men to share the splendours that lay within, splendours including the Victoria Falls Hotel, where the three of us were, five minutes ago, being yelled at by an exceptionally vexatious black security guard in a lime-green uniform.

So they called it Rhodesland. Then they changed it to Rhodesia. He was over the moon.

'Has anyone else had a country called after their name?' he hollered, jubilantly. 'Now I don't care what they do to me!'

And now, less than a hundred years later, a young man is about to be elected in to the South African parliament called Mandla 'Ka' Shabandu. 'Ka' Shabandu was on Death Row at Robben Island for blowing up an oil-refinery as part of the ANC's clandestine war against the settlers. He was reprieved at the last minute. 'Ka' is short for Kalashnikov, his favourite type of gun. Just three weeks from now, Trevor will be governed by people who name themselves after choice weaponry. No wonder he's denying knowledge of the very existence of apartheid. I know I would. Fuck it: if John Prescott, on the eve of an election victory, abruptly changed his name to 'AK47'

Prescott, I'd be the first to hide my Telecom shares at the bottom of the underwear drawer.

———

I must point out, at this juncture, I've never been a keen traveller. I've never subscribed to the school of thought that suggests holidays should constitute some sort of endurance test – like those ebullient people who tell you what an eye-opening experience it was to unicycle through Patagonia and get scurvy, jump into rapids and eat biltong.

I've never, for instance, felt the yearning to follow in the footsteps of my more dissatisfied friends, and go off to Thailand to discover myself. God forbid. What would I find? (The closest my friends got to bringing back a fragment of Eastern culture, by the way, was purchasing enough Vietnamese wicker wall hangings to transform their Putney maisonettes into the set of the *Deer Hunter*. But that's liberalism for you – all the trappings, none of the Russian Roulette).

I had considered it once before. Thinking, momentarily, that I *was* dissatisfied, I attended the recruitment day of a voluntary aid organization called Christians Overseas (which, if you ask me, is the best place for them). But they rejected me on the grounds that they'd had eighty thousand applications for seven-hundred-and-fifty places. It was a rare spectacle: watching thousands of fresh-faced seventeen-year-olds pleading with total strangers to let them have a crap time for two years.

'Please,' they begged, 'let us catch dysentery and live in a woad hut two thousand miles from the nearest Seven-Eleven. You don't even have to pay us.' But entry was strict, and you were disqualified on the grounds of possessing – amongst other things – elderly relatives, children, bank debts, and pending divorce cases. I ask you: why *else* would anyone want to bugger off to the Third World? Can you really imagine anyone declaring, 'I'm in a marvellous, dependent-free relationship, and I've got a healthy bank balance. I think I'll move to Somalia.' People don't *move* to the Third World. They *escape* there.

And anyway, ever since the Michael Jackson debacle, I've

———

been dubious of the motives of anyone who wants to spend so much of their free time Healing The World. We're simply not that bounteous: it's not in our nature. This isn't altruism. It's denial. I'm waiting for the time when charitable endeavours are officially recognized by psychiatrists as being symptoms. I'm waiting to find out what Anita Roddick has been hiding all these years.

Now I no longer have any time for the War Is Hell brigade – all those Vietnam vets you read about in the papers who get all dressed up in combat gear, shoot everybody in Pizza Huts, and blame it on the fact that they spent a year in a Viet Cong water pit being bitten by rats. I have experienced war now, and it is nothing compared to the unbridled horror of an overland camping safari group fun holiday.

If this vacation of mine ever manifests itself in post-traumatic stress syndrome, my Bophuthatswanian experience will have nothing to do with it. No. It will indubitably materialize in an uncontrollable hankering to hang around Youth Hostel Associations and smash innocent bystanders over the head with a calor gas stove, or track down boisterous gung-ho Australian backpackers and garotte them to death with a set of tent-pegs.

—

I said my goodbyes to Trevor and Doug the next day, and flew back to Harare where I'd arranged to meet up with Jungle Tours, the overland safari adventure fun holiday people. From the moment I got out of the taxi at the Cresta Lodge Campsite, murmurings of unease began to bubble in the pit of my stomach.

Let me begin by introducing you to the group: I shall call the two Australians who sit in front of me Miss Native American Indian Healing Technique and Miss Pagan Goddess of Soil Rapture. Maybe that'll get confusing. Okay, I'll call them Sturdy Dyke One and Sturdy Dyke Two. They are strangely silent. Sturdy Dyke One spends each day recording authentic African street noises on her tape recorder and plays them back quietly to herself in the bus, while smiling serenely. Sturdy Dyke Two says nothing for hours, and suddenly – the moment

—

we pass a mud hut or an exquisite sunset – yells, 'PHOTO STOP', leaps out, and snaps away a roll of film on her Kodak Instamatic.

Sitting behind me are two fifteen-year-olds going through strange hormonal changes they don't quite understand. I shall call them Young Mister Hormonal Change One and Young Mister Hormonal Change Two. Young Mister Hormonal Change One has discovered a band called Rage Against The Machine and insists on relentlessly quoting me lines from their songs to illustrate whatever event occurs. Thus: we're driving through a savanna, and some baboon throws a rock at the bus, and Young Mister Hormonal Change One says, 'Wow! It's just like that song when he goes "Fuck You I Won't Do What You Tell Me".' And he bangs his head up and down.

Then there is Group Leader Stewart who remembers the words to more Supertramp songs than – one assumes (and hopes, for the sake of their wives) – Supertramp themselves. He doesn't just know the words – he's also familiar with the drum patterns. When he isn't crashing his hands up and down on the dashboard, Stewart says things like, 'Let's just bibble into town,' and 'Keep your wallets in your sweaty little mitts,' and 'If you give me $5 then we're squitz.'

There are others – 'Anna', an enthusiastic Scandinavian who is deeply in favour of all climatic changes.

'Rain,' she says. 'Wind, sun, snow. They're all the same to me. They're all a part of God's beauty.'

There's a German man and wife who don't talk. I shall call the wife Steffi because that is the only female German name I can think of apart from Claudia, which is her real name. Steffi shakes a lot, and is vehemently, personally offended by the lack of tread on my walking shoes.

'You'll fall off the rocks,' she says. 'You'll fall, you know. You should have bought *my* brand: "I'm A Sanctimonious Outdoor Imbecile Shoes".' Or something like that. I've stopped listening by now. I am planning my escape.

———

Our basic itinerary is this: we drive for eight hours a day through Zimbabwe's dullest grassland listening to *Breakfast In*

———

America and *The Golden Hour Of Supertramp*. Every so often, we get out of the bus, climb a large mountain to look at a ruin, say, 'Mmm, old,' and then drive two hundred miles before parking at a lay-by cum rubbish dump. It is dark by now, so we hit our thumbs with a mallet while trying to hammer a tent-peg into concrete. Then we take it in turns to cook supper, build a fire, and sing 'Why Must I Be A Teenager In Love'.

Stewart then performs his nightly lecture, which consists of variations on the following themes:

1. All indigenous Zimbabwe residents are thieves, and will stop at nothing to plunder our tent-pegs and sell them on the black market for food and cigarettes.

2. If we let the tent-pegs out of our sight for a moment, we'll be held personally responsible for their replacement cost.

3. We're all having the most marvellous time, and will continue to do so.

Bearing in mind that Stewart calls tent-pegs (I can barely bring myself to write this) 'tent-y-peg-pegs', you get the picture. Being given a lecture on equipment security by Stewart is not unlike being given a lecture on first aid by Kermit the Frog's nephew.

Stewart loves apes. Indeed, he loves apes to the extent that he assures me that coming face to face with our primate cousins can trigger off an astonishing cognitive reaction, a deep inner creativity that we subconsciously suppressed when we stopped being monkeys and started going to restaurants.

In fact, Stewart takes this philosophy so far that he spends a sizable chunk of his free time going 'ooh ooh ooh' and lolloping around in a field on his elbows. He has studied these creatures for so long now that he claims to be able to actually talk ape talk, to chat with simians about this and that.

'What I'm saying in baboon talk,' he explains on the third evening, 'is "leave me alone". That's "*ugh* ugh ugh", whereas "ugh *ugh* ugh" is "come any closer to my food and I'll kill you".'

'Don't you sometimes feel,' I say, 'that we look upon our simian cousins with rose-tinted spectacles?'

'Oh no,' says Stewart. 'Oh no.'

'They're not, let's face it, scintillating conversationists,' I say.

'Yes they are,' replies Stewart, grinning, gesticulating energetically, as if I've just put my finger on the hub of the riddle. 'They are scintillating conversationists – in their way! You see? Ha!'

The next morning, I awake to discover that our campsite is terrifyingly situated in the direct path of large oncoming vehicles, just three miles away from a charming little village where comely, beaming hoteliers charge $10 a night for a sumptuous meal, a hot bath and a huge double bed.

'Why?' I say to Stewart at this point. 'Why did we sleep on a road? Why?'

And he replies, 'This is an African *adventure*. Come on everyone, let's bibble on out of here.'

So we do. We drive into more grassland, through quaint villages where, in an energizing display of hands-across-the-ocean cultural unity, the entire community (tribal elders, beaming children, ladies with washing on their heads) gather at the roadside to point and chuckle at the bus.

In return, we throw sweets out of the window, hitting small boys on the head, while Stewart cranks up the engine and drives away, coating the lot of them in a noxious haze of red dust, wiping the smiles off their faces once and for all. This basic schedule continues for four whole days, right through the Botswana border, until we pitch camp in Maun.

––––––

Maun, Botswana, is one of the few remaining bastions of darkest, whitest Africa, the last of the great frontier towns. Just two years ago, a lengthy, hazardous dirt track was the only means of approach, besides an exclusive airport that catered solely for big game hunters and their elegant, rickety four-seater charter planes. Dusty men sat in bars and discussed the previous day's kill.

Now the road is tarmacked, which pisses everyone off, popular opinion being that, any second, thousands of fresh-faced Scandinavians are about to hurl themselves into the

––––––

pool area armed with their lilos, their Sidney Sheldon books and their libertarian, do-gooder ways.

And their concerns have grounding. Campsites for paupers are cropping up all over the place. The town is just beginning to be deluged by mellow tye-dye hippies wandering around saying 'wow' a lot, and sunburnt gung-ho outdoor types clutching herds of intricately carved giant wooden giraffes. (The country's economy appears to be wholly based on the unfathomable logic that European holidaymakers have a desperate urge to purchase these finely constructed – but altogether awful – beasts the moment they land in a hot country.)

The Island Safari hippie camp and Oddballs Campsite have opened, and the latter's advertisement portrays – terrifyingly – a spaced-out hippie smoking a joint amongst much psychedelic idiocy. There is a cultural battle going on: the big game hunters versus the hippie conservationist versus the mud hut dwellers who are perfectly content to stand by trees and cultivate goats without Pagan Goddess Of Soil Rapture types running in and informing them how terrific they are.

It is Friday evening when Jungle Tours blunders into Island Safari.

'Okey dokey,' says Stewart, turning off the Tina Turner cassette. 'We're home. Who's on table and stool duty tonight?'

'ME!' yells Sturdy Dyke Two, and skips dutifully out of the bus.

'Jon,' continues Stewart. 'You're cook wallah tonight. What's gonna be hot off the stove?'

'Nice toast tonight,' I reply. 'Nice toast with lovely butter.'

'Mmmm,' says Anna. 'Nice toast.'

Yawning, I stretch and glance out of the window. We are not alone. The camp appears to have been overrun by the Manson Family. Many brightly coloured love children (and love middle-agers) are grooving along gently and (I think this is the correct term) 'freaking' each other 'out'.

'Paranoia!' shrieks one man, chasing his friend through the park. 'Paranoia!' he giggles.

'No! No!,' replies his friend, who is, it appears, having a bad trip. 'Noooooo!!!'

'Damn my eyes,' I groan to myself. 'Damn them all to hell.'

——

Now I can stand it no longer. The anxiety is digging its way into my mind, altering my very essence in subtle, awful ways. Earlier this evening, while I was cleaning the stove, Anna asked me if I needed any help. 'Okey-dokey,' I replied. I didn't say, 'Yes, please.' I said 'Okey-dokey.' I had to physically stop myself from saying, 'Okey-dokey-hippety-hop.' That's what I *wanted* to say. That's what my brain was telling me to say.

And, with a start, I was hit by the ominous truth. I am turning into the Patty Hearst of African adventure fun holidays, my memories of fashionable London society evaporating irrevocably. I am becoming merely a thing that sleeps in tents, a thing that cooks for fifteen with boundless enthusiasm.

My initial paranoia, before embarking on the trip, was that I'd fall victim to Kaspar Hauser Syndrome: that I'd somehow become isolated from the group in the middle of the bush, and they'd find me in fifteen years walking around on all fours. But now I realize that a much more fearful, and tenable fate may befall me: that I might become a full-time robust and hardy person – taking up juggling, travelling around the world working in bars, learning how to play 'All You Have To Do Is Dream' on a traditional wooden instrument.

At 4.00 a.m., I scramble startledly from my sleeping bag, indubitably convinced that my tent-pegs are about to be shanghaied by vicious, scheming locals. I had abandoned three or four in a small bag about ten feet from the tent, and there is only one thought in my mind: they must be rescued. My tent-pegs have become more like children than camping equipment to me these past few days, and their safety is foremost in my mind.

So, armed with a can of insect repellent (for spraying in the bandits' eyes) and a rubber torch, I creep out from underneath the canvas. There is no question in my mind that the enemy are within feet. I'm not certain who they are: possibly a crack scout outfit of ANC activists, maybe Mandla 'Ka' Shabandu himself, skulking through the undergrowth, eager to

——

humiliate me in many awful ways, steal the tent-pegs, get me into trouble with Stewart, whose admonishment is certain to be trenchant and cute at the same time – invariably the most formidable form of admonishment.

The outside world is eerily silent. A campfire that was – just a few hours ago – being danced around by vigorous youngsters is now glowing with its final dying embers. The stars are huge tonight – far huger than they are in Britain, but more or less the same thing. It is the crack of dawn, and here I am in a field in the middle of the southern hemisphere clutching a large torch with which to frenziedly bludgeon a mob of nonexistent political foe to protect what are basically – emotional attachments apart – small bits of metal. This is the final straw, I think ruefully. This is not how it was meant to be.

It is at this moment that I make the snap decision to jump ship, change tack, and so on. I must get myself to a big city – any city – with all its smell and noise and pretty girls and limitless urban possibilities. Enough of this infernal bush-living.

Temporarily slumming it in unmanageable undergrowth had seemed a splendid idea when I was back in London, sipping from a large Bloody Mary, where the nearest unmanageable undergrowth was miles away in somewhere awful like Devon. But I am a city boy, and a city is where I must go.

And then I hit upon New York. I have a wealthy cousin in the entertainment industry who's always promising to initiate me into his glamorous ways, take me to the finest parties, introduce me to Madonna's dancers – that sort of thing. And New York really knows how to treat its members of the entertainment industry well. When, for instance, they gave Nelson Mandela a tickertape celebration parade through the streets of Manhattan, they had Mrs Cosby from *The Cosby Show* resplendent in an open-top limousine leading the cortége. Now *that's* classy! You wouldn't get that in fuddy-duddy old Britain. We'd *never* have the ladies from, say, *Birds of a Feather* greeting, say, Vaclav Havel at the airport while on a state visit. We're far too crusty and near-sighted for that. And that, I contend, is Britain's loss.

6

'It's a wonderful concept for a book,' says Cunard.

'Wonderful because it's *true*,' I reply. 'The QE2 *deserves* it. I'm thinking of calling it *High Class – Affordable Prices. The Queen Sails Onwards And Henceforth*.'

'Are you writing about any other cruise liners?' says Cunard.

'Well I guess that I have to because the publishers want there to be comparisons, but quite frankly I don't see the point. There's only one QE2.'

'Absolutely.'

'It's like doing a book on the Royal Family, and comparing the Queen with another Queen who lives in Basildon. Queen Canberra who lives in a little pebble-dash council house in Essex with an outside toilet. Whats the point?'

'There *is* only one Queen.'

'And there's only one QE2.'

There is a slightly chagrined, reluctantly embarrassed pause at this point, before he speaks again.

'I don't want to tell you what to write,' he says, shyly, slowly, 'but if we *are* going to give you a free trip, it's important you should know that we're trying to explode the myth that the QE2 is just for affluent widows and the super-rich.'

'That's exactly the myth that I'm trying to explode too. The book is going to be for the youngsters. I'm going to write it in a very "in your face" style. You know, the QE2 as a ship of fun, where boys and girls can forge relationships.'

'I'm not sure about "in your face".'

'Well not totally *in* the face. Not all the way *inside*. I mean . . .' I pause. 'But you know as well as I do that there just aren't that many rich widows about any more.'

And Cunard fall for the ruse hook, line and sinker, as the old nautical expression goes. Penning *Onwards And Henceforth* is, of course, the last thing on my mind, and getting to New York is the first.

'You want a new life?' my wealthy showbiz cousin Joel had said to me on the phone. 'You want to meet the stars and dine in the best restaurants? You want to get out of dying, funny little Britain?'

'Yes!' I yelled.

'Then get yourself to New York!'

———

Many, many years ago – before I was born – my aunt concluded that London life was dull and stifling. So one day, on the spur of the moment, she decided to buy herself a map of the world, set it down on the floor, close her eyes, throw a pebble, and blindly journey to whichever foreign soil the fates determined. She was only seventeen years old. These were the days when seventeen-year-olds didn't do that sort of thing. Nonetheless, she threw the stone, and it landed on India. The very next day she packed her bags and didn't come home for seven years.

There's a couple of days to kill before the QE2 sets sail to New York, and the prospect of simply wasting my time away in London staring at the clock is too much to bear. As I sit in my flat now, with a world globe perched enticingly on my desk, it suddenly dawns on me how thrilling that moment must have been for my aunt: placing her destiny in the hands of the gods, denying herself the fundamental liberty to choose the path of her future. But then I think, fuck it, I'd probably end up in Belgium. So I catch the next plane to Prague.

———

I have, it transpires, picked something of a sparkling week to come to this most beautiful and ancient of Eastern European cities. General Pinochet, Prince Charles – 'The King Of Wales' – Aerosmith and Boutros Boutros Ghali are all in town, and it is a media frenzy. Pinochet, Charles and Aerosmith are being trailed everywhere they go by zealous stringers, eager for a few choice quotes about arms dealing, baroque architecture, and life on the road being just one hotel room after another. Poor old Boutros Boutros, however, is being shunned by the crowd, and I can't help feeling sorry for him.

Poor guy: he's had it tough all along. If your name was Mrs Boutros Ghali, would *you* go and call your kid 'Boutros'?

———

What kind of mean-spirited parent would play that cheap trick on her son? And now his thunder is being all but stolen by the Aerosmith cortège, screaming through the crumbling streets in their tantalizing white limousines. For every five journalists excitedly chasing the band through the town, there's one lacklustre correspondent mumbling the odd polite inanity to the UN Secretary General.

And I am one of those polite mumblers, I'm sorry to say. I had rather hoped to get in on the Aerosmith freebie myself. A British heavy metal magazine has promised to refund my air ticket if I can deliver an interview with the band. But the man at the Czech press-centre didn't speak good English, and when I said 'Aerosmith' he made the wholly understandable error of thinking I'd actually said 'Boutros Boutros Ghali'. Consequently, I was directed here to the UN press assembly.

This is a worry. Aerosmith are in town for another seventy hours, and if I miss them my only course of action will be to change tack and try and get hold of another Major Celebrity to take their place. And believe me, convincing *Kerrang!* to run a two-page feature on General Pinochet will be a bugger.

I came to Prague because I was curious to see the high life in its infancy – a tourist industry that has had just five years to flourish since the collapse of Communism. Getting to Aerosmith, I admit, will be a pleasant bonus, but not my primary objective.

In South Africa I had seen a high society running scared: Mandela's impending election victory casting an ominous shadow over the white man's fun, like a reprimanding adult back home early from a twenty-seven-year holiday and catching the kids trashing the place. In Prague, the parents have abandoned home for good, given the kids the keys to the car, and not even left a forwarding address.

I wanted to see how they were dealing with their new-found responsibility, whether they were keeping the place tidy and the fridge stocked. And whether, indeed, they were being chivalrous towards their house-guests. I mention this extra-ordinarily sparkling metaphor to Bob, the journalist sitting next to me at the Boutros Boutros jamboree, and he replies,

'What are you doing tonight? I'll take you somewhere, Jon, that'll make your hair stand on end.'

'Where's that, Bob?' I reply. (I was, in fact, intending to see one of those Czech plays about a man whose nose gets confiscated by the Communists and then turns up in his wife's soup, but I was secretly hoping that a better offer would come my way.)

'Just you wait,' says Bob. 'You want to see how Prague is coping with its new-found freedom? I'll show you.'

Bob is a handsome man from Washington DC, with the sort of looks that win presidential elections: Robert Redford eyes, Robert Redford cheekbones. One can imagine him back home, joyfully constructing shelving units, hunting elk, riding around the backyard on a bicycle without brakes, cracking the Watergate cover-up, and so on. Like many of the older American expatriates, Bob came here straight after the Velvet Revolution to 'live out my mid-life crisis'. He was hoping to find some peace here, an easy life amidst the optimism and joy of a youthful democracy. 'And you know what, Jon,' he says. 'I *have* found that joy. And it's here. All around us.'

'Where?'

'Here, Jon.' And he waves his arms all about.

There's something strange going on here at the Garden Club Eden, but I don't know what it is. Bob won't tell me why he's brought me here – why he's chosen this place as opposed to fifty other over-priced seventies shoddy erotic emporiums around Wenceslas Square, Prague's answer to Piccadilly Circus.

It is a hell of a place, Wenceslas Square: hippie-chick American beatniks with black leather jackets and their goateed boyfriends singing Leonard Cohen songs out of tune, offering to plait my hair for the price of a beer – 'Come on, man, this is Prague! Let your hair down' – giving me an insight into what must have been going through Nixon's mind when he sent the troops into Kent State. The beatniks have adopted Prague as their second home because this is the city that made Frank Zappa Cultural Affairs attaché (what next? My Little

Pony as Minister for Sport?), a president who punctuates his autograph with a little heart, Semtex, the Skoda and Kafka – all the things that beatniks love the most.

In the alleyways around the Square (which isn't a square, if truth be told, it's a street) overweight Germans fondle under-age hookers, gratefully accepting fellatio in the brisk, chilly evening wind. The concept of outdoor sex is wholly alien to me, by the way. Call me repressed, but I cannot imagine ever being able to convince Little Johnny Penis to unslump himself from the warm, soft mattress of my inner thigh in such an alfresco environment. But judging by the happy grunts of the German businessmen who were banging away in back alleys all around us as we walked into the club, I guess that I'm alone in this inability to copulate amongst the elements. I don't know. Maybe they just close their eyes and imagine that they're Heathcliff in *Wuthering Heights*.

But more than anything, Wenceslas Square is home to costly floor shows starring dour women in feathered bikinis, going through the motions, looking as if nobody has informed them that Communism is over and that they are, therefore, allowed to take the Regulation Sullen Expressions off their faces that were mandatory under the regime.

The Garden Club Eden appears, at first, to bear no significant distinction from the rest of these establishments. It nestles below a hairdresser's, with all the cosy charm of a tawdry erotic sauna bar in Dalston called Elite Lovely Ladies, or something. Slick-suited oily Germans with hefty gold cufflinks lounge casually on the sofas like dozens of Tony Blairs. The drinks are overpriced, and the buffet looks ready to get up and dance as soon as a song it knows the words to comes on.

The building itself, however, is beautiful and baroque, like almost every other building in the magnificently archaic town centre. The explanation for this abundance of loveliness is that the people of Prague, historically pacifist by nature, had hastily capitulated to the Nazis before a single bomb was dropped on the place. Consequently, the architecture survived intact. Unfortunately, the Jews did not. But aesthetes are a hardcore bunch, and, when attractive buildings are at stake, sometimes there's just no talking to them.

Perhaps I am being a trifle unfair. It would be wrong, I think, to imply that the people of Prague went as far as to sell the Jews out. That would infer a certain amount of aggressiveness on their part, and these people wouldn't know aggressiveness if it went up to them and punched them in the face.

'They are so passive here,' explains Bob, 'that until last year the waiters were still putting "reserved" signs on the tables so they didn't have to serve anybody.'

These magnificent fairytale edifices outlived forty-odd years of Communist rule too – they just built huge slabs of concrete on the remaining free space. If you can imagine a magnificent gargantuan Hansel and Gretel theme park slap-bang in the middle of industrial Gwent, then that's pretty much Prague.

We have been in the club for three hours now, and nothing perceptibly symbolic of a society unshackled from the burden of totalitarianism has so far occurred. Bob is being annoyingly coy about the whole business, and I'm beginning to wonder if I'm wasting my time. The hours are ticking away on the Aerosmith front, and my expenses are rising.

'Just wait till the floor show starts,' says Bob. 'Just you wait. This is going to be *special*. What's the time?'

'Midnight.'

'Any second now. Any second . . .'

The lights go out, and we are in darkness.

'Just watch this,' whispers Bob. 'This is it.'

Onto the stage walks a woman in her early thirties, entirely naked except for a Russian peaked cap and a fake AK47 covering her crotch. The music begins. It is Pink Floyd's 'Another Brick In The Wall'. When it gets to the bit about not wanting any thought control, the lady aims the gun at the audience and pretends to shoot.

'Whooo-hooo!' yells Bob, standing up on his chair. 'Yeah. Shoot me, babe. Give it to me between the eyes.'

'What the hell is this?' I ask.

'This is the Czechs getting back at the Communists,'

----

replies Bob, laughing. And he throws his arms into the air and yells, 'AND WHAT A WAY TO GET BACK AT THEM!'

We order some more drinks, and the floor show continues.

'Just wait 'til you see the S&M act,' says Bob, nudging me in the ribs. 'This is the best part. People ask me why I live here. This is why. Here it is now . . .'

On the stage two young ladies shackled together with manacles shuffle towards the gun lady, who points her weapon menacingly at their faces. The music stops and the soundtrack cuts to a deep, sinister voice announcing: 'Workers Of The World Unite, You Have Nothing To Lose But Your Chains.'

The ladies do, indeed, lose their chains, which fall clunking to the floor. Now wholly unclothed, they squeal and run around a bit. Then the three of them bow, and the stage goes black. Bob and I clap.

'Hubba hubba,' says Bob. 'Communista Erotika. Come on. You ain't seen nothing yet.'

'What do you mean, Bob?' I reply.

'Come on, Jon,' he says. 'We're going up into the hills.'

'Okay,' I reply, eager for an excuse for not returning to my sad hotel room. 'Let's go.'

———

Let me tell you about my sad hotel room. After much negotiation, one of the expensive, privately owned boarding houses in the town centre had offered me a few free nights bed and breakfast. I was grateful, of course, the room would normally have cost over £150 a night. But I discovered on arrival that the place was drab and drafty, little more than a youth hostel. A previous resident had scrawled on the wall with red paint, and my toilet door was hanging off its hinges.

But even getting this had been a struggle. Under Communism, of course, Prague had grown up with no concept of self-promotion. Even now, the posters promoting the strip shows around Wenceslas Square exhibit photographs of the REAL LADIES that you are about to see naked – in glorious colour – stretch marks and moustaches intact. It is comforting to see

———

such honesty, but equally remarkable to witness such a poor grasp of market forces.

Go to London's strip clubs – for instance – and hanging, framed, on the door are seductive photographs of Elizabeth Hurley or Patsy Kensit with their legs alluringly akimbo and their eyes inviting you hither.

Horniness being a far more powerful emotion than logic, you rush inside the club persuading yourself that Ms Hurley must be earning some extra pocket money between fashion assignments, and you take your seat to discover that the lady on the stage looks remarkably like your great-aunt, and that the climax of her act is when she tantalizingly unravels the loose skin from underneath her armpit.

By now, of course, you have paid your money, and if you complain to the management that their posters contravene the fair trading laws, they will almost certainly offer to hit you over the head with a mallet and write to your mother informing her that her son enjoys nothing better than to spend his evenings watching a stage act entitled 'Lesbian Lavatory Lust'. This is Western capitalism at its most dynamic, and a concept that the Czechs haven't come to terms with yet.

No. And similarily, the Prague tourist industry hasn't quite grasped the minutiae of self-publicity. Convincing the hotels to offer me a free room in return for a write up in my book had been like trying to sell a copy of *Women Who Love Too Much* to Myra Hindley.

'Let me get this straight,' said the manager of the fifth hotel I had telephoned. 'You are researching a book about Prague, and if we give you a free room, you will *write* about the room, which, in turn, will convince others to stay in the room. Is that right?'

'Yes,' I said.

'Well I never!' she exclaimed. 'Well. Okay then!'

But, as I say, the room is drab and depressing, and even though it is beginning to dawn on me that Bob is quite patently psychotic, I gladly agree to allow him to escort me into the hills above the city.

―――
―――

Our next stop is Club Communista, an S&M emporium situated at a 'secret location' in the hills above the city, which doesn't turn out to be all that secret, because there are huge signs everywhere saying 'CLUB COMMUNISTA – PRAHA 9' and every policeman we ask (Bob is a little hazy about the location) happily points us in the right direction, all of which impairs the clandestine thrill somewhat. Call me old-fashioned, but I like my Communista Erotika S&M clubs to be covert, and not signposted. I want to be able to knock three times and ask for 'Vladimir, Fuck Slave of Stalingrad'. Our trip tonight is panning out like an excursion to the Ideal Home Exhibition.

We arrive eventually at a sign on the door that reads, in three different languages: 'Sexy Communist Clothing Necessary For S&M Room', which pretty much counts me out – I am wearing a rather nice casual jacket and slacks tonight. And anyway, some people look terrific in a furry Russian hat with a large steel girder sticking out of their penis, but not me, I'm sorry to report. Vaclav the doorman, however, does.

He is wearing torn leather jeans, a black leather jacket emblazoned with the Russian flag, and a handlebar moustache hefty enough to clothe Somalia, if knitted correctly. He looks fabulous – well, fabulous in comparison to the majority of the city's other security guards and doormen, who spend their days all dressed up like Buttons from Mother Goose in powdered grey wigs and sky-blue doublets and hose. Okay, we have our official fancy dress in London too, but they are prohibited from standing anywhere except for Buckingham Palace and the Tower. Here in Prague they are *everywhere* – hovering forlornly like lost extras from *Amadeus* outside every museum and minor ministerial building. I can't help thinking that it is something of a poorly conceived scheme. How will they cope in the event of an attack? Fan the enemy into submission? Play them harpsichord solos until they come quietly?

'Bob,' yells Vaclav the doorman, in faltering English. 'My main man!'

'Vaclav!' yells Bob back. 'Meet my good friend, Jon!'

'Jon!' yells Vaclav. 'How are you doing?'

'Vaclav!' I yell back. 'Fine, thanks!'

'Hey you guys,' says Vaclav, 'the floor show is starting in the swimming pool in forty-five minutes. You just go in there and have yourselves a good time.'

'How much money do you want?' I say.

'Jon, Jon, my man. Any friend of Bob . . . You just go and have yourself some fun.'

We thank Vaclav, and head straight into the S&M bar: portentous, blackened shutters, huge, leather-clad truckers leaning menacingly at the bar while handlebar moustaches with torn jeans saunter up and down the corridors.

Bob suggests that I pay special attention to the handkerchiefs, for they play a vital part in the complex S&M mating ritual, each colour – red, yellow and brown – signifying the preferred bodily emission to be imbibed during love-making. And I think: how different is this world. In *my* world, I just walk up to the woman I fancy and pant vigorously.

Consequently I avoid the toilets, assuming that, as we speak, large groups of frightening construction engineers are crammed into the cubicles mutually leaping up and down on each others' scrotums while whooping with glee. But all is not what it seems. If you go up close and listen in to conversations, you're more likely to hear the clientele discussing the idiosyncracies of the latest production of *Die Fledermaus* than arranging an evening involving the collective superglueing of nipples to passing Intercity 125s.

'Look at that terrifying skinhead,' I say to Bob, 'I wouldn't like to meet him in a darkened alley.'

'He runs a florists near Charles Bridge,' he replies.

'Look at *him*,' I say. 'I've never seen anyone quite so fierce-looking in my life.'

'Ah,' says Bob. 'He's got a little bistro in the old town.' And so on.

Out of the corner of my eye, I notice two naked women rubbing each other down with body oil, a small crowd gathered around. They don't appear to be employees of the club: just a couple of young, local women, living out their new found liberty. I tut, contemplate how lamentable it is that some people feel forced to declare their sexuality in so public an arena, ponder upon how wretched some of us become when nourished with the gift of freedom. And I head to the bar to get myself a drink.

'Ah,' says Bob. 'A sight for sore eyes. Eh Jon?'

'Yeah,' I reply, distracted.

'What's wrong?'

'Well, I'm a little worried, Bob,' I reply. 'I wasn't supposed to be at the Boutros Boutros Ghali press conference today. I'm supposed to be covering the Aerosmith visit, and if I don't get an interview, I'll have to pay for my own flight home.'

We walk over to a wooden bench near a huge oak crucifix that leans against the wall, and sit down between five men dressed – more or less – from head to toe in rubber and leather.

'You're trying to get hold of Aerosmith, huh?' says Bob.

'Yes.'

'Well, you know something, Jon. I think I can help you. Just you wait here.'

Bob stands up and rushes off to speak to Vaclav. I busy myself by contemplating how lamentable the two naked women are for another five minutes or so, before my attention is distracted by a lady placing a snake in her rectum on a small stage at the back of the bar.

'Well that certainly is lamentable too,' I murmur to myself, looking back at the two oily ladies, trying to work out which of the three are the most lamentable of all.

Just as I conclude that there's really nothing in it, and that they are equally lamentable, a lady dressed entirely in bright-red rubber saunters into the room clutching a large horsewhip. She walks over to the bench, speaks quietly to the man sitting next-but-one to me. I crane to overhear the conversation, but it is far too quiet. Eventually, the man nods sombrely, and allows himself to be led towards the crucifix. Then, slowly, and surprisingly gently, she begins to whip him: three soft whips, followed by a hard one, the entire transaction repeated three or four times.

After a while, the man, suitably chastised, thanks her, and re-takes his place on the bench. Then the lady repeats the exchange to the man sitting next to me. A few words, a nod, and a whipping. I watch transfixed, wholly – and dimwittedly – unaware of the considerably obvious fact that this is the bench set aside for the potential whippees, and that I am next in line. For a moment later, the lady approaches me, and whispers something in Czech in my ear.

'I'm sorry?' I say.

'Ah, English,' she replies. 'Have you been, um, how do I say it? Ah! Have you been a naughty boy?'

The question comes as such a shock – such a bolt from the blue – that I have absolutely no idea how to respond.

'Well,' I reply, stuttering, 'I suppose that depends on what you classify as being "naughty".'

'What?'

I guess that I've been sort of naughty,' I continue stupidly, 'but not what you'd call . . . Ah. Oh. Right. I see.'

But it is too late. The lady glares angrily at me and moves on to the next man, who has been, it appears, extraordinarily naughty, for the two of them immediately rush off to the crucifix. I breathe a sigh of relief. At that moment, Bob returns with a tall, denim-clad American man in tow.

Bob,' I say, 'you wouldn't believe what has just happened to me.'

'Jon,' he replies breathlessly, 'I'd like you to meet somebody.'

'Hi!' The man extends his hand. 'Bob's told me a lot about you.'

'Really?' I say.

This,' says Bob, with a look of triumph in his face, 'is Frank.'

'Good to meet you,' says Frank, brushing his long, blond tousled hair away from his face.

'Hi Frank,' I say.

'Frank,' continues Bob, 'is very heavily connected with a certain band you've been hoping to meet.'

'Really?' I say.

'That's right,' says Frank, and he gives me a big grin. 'That's right,' he says, after a moment. 'I am the lead guitarist of Aerosmith.'

What must life in Prague have been like during the last days of Communism? A man called Greg famously painted a tank pink. The jail where Vaclav Havel was imprisoned by the Secret Service was also painted pink, turned into a theme hotel. (To what extremes the hotel owners take the theme, by the way, I have no idea. Are the guests fed prison food? Locked in their rooms at 10.00 p.m.? Raped by a waiter dressed as a Mexican armed robber in the showers before breakfast?)

Everywhere, hippie splinter groups and solemn fringe theatre outfits made dumb gestures on a huge scale – mass face paintings and political mime – kind of like the Glastonbury Festival with the possibility of getting tear-gassed.

Even now, amongst all the McDonalds and the Trusthouse Fortes, the people of Prague have retained much of their dippy idealistic fervour. When a big American conglomerate purchased a popular restaurant and promptly announced that they were going to close it for two years for refurbishment, outrage amongst the people was so rampant that Havel himself had to intervene. Eventually, a group of irate locals forced the doors open and began to redistribute the liquor in return for voluntary donations.

Curiously, Prague still hasn't been besieged by drugs, even though the city is now a recognized transit point between Turkey and Western Europe. The Prague-born youngsters are too poor to purchase drugs, and there's nothing much to steal. All the valuable artworks are painted on ceilings, and it's tough enough getting a dope dealer to accept a cheque, let alone an opera house.

In fact, Bob tells me, the vast majority of Prague's drug consumption takes place within the sub-culture of the rich American beatnik backpackers, and the only drug of note being guzzled is LSD. And – as far as the drugs/breakdown of society equation goes – acid is relatively innocuous (apart from the very tenable peril of innocent bystanders being hit on the head by flocks of wingless, tye-dye clad adolescents plummeting from rooftops while hastily re-evaluating their aviatory skills). While crack's rather troublesome side effect is turning its recipient into Fredrick West and his wife, the closest you'll get to acid-related ferocity is when your brain explodes and you spend the rest of your life hiding in the bathroom. So for now, anyway, the city is safe.

Frank, the lead guitarist from Aerosmith, tells me that he spent much of his time here in Prague around the time of the Velvet Revolution, giving celebrity lectures to clandestine anarchist groups.

'We weren't fighting for democracy. We were fighting for the death of *all* leadership. Society is in such a terrible state all over the world. For instance, women's education is *never* geared towards highly paid jobs. And do you know why?' He peers at me over his fringe. I shrug.

'It's because all the teachers are male.'

I think about this for a minute, and decide to go with it. 'I know what you mean,' I say.

'I've got a kidney complaint,' he continues. 'Every month, I have to go to the doctor to get medicine for my kidneys. And don't you understand the implications of what I'm telling you?'

'Um,' I say.

'SOCIETY,' he replies, 'HAS TAKEN CONTROL OF MY BODY.'

There is a long pause.

'It's a terrible thing,' says Bob.

'And that,' concludes Frank, 'is the sort of thing I told the anarchist groups that asked me to lecture them.'

'It must have been tough fitting celebrity lectures into your busy workday schedule.'

'It was,' says Frank. 'Of course, when we were touring or making albums, I had to cut down on the lectures because the band always comes first.'

'Do you get unnecessarily bothered by fans?'

'Sometimes, yes.'

'Which is the very favourite of all your albums?'

'Well, you know, I always think that the last album is the best. It's the closest to my heart. But I do have a very special fondness for our very first album.'

'How was your last album received?'

'Very well.'

'Was it a departure?'

———

'Yes.'

'What's your surname?'

'Um, Crowley.'

'Are you happy?'

'I know it's an old cliché, but happiness really is a very subjective concept.'

So for the next forty-five minutes or so, my questions and Frank's answers are volleyed around like a tennis match between the Care Bears, while Bob looks on with ill-disguised pride.

'I bet you never thought I could fix *this*, eh?' he says, while Frank goes to the toilet.

'I'm certainly surprised,' I agree. 'How do you know him?'

'Ah, you know. I have my sources.'

By now, of course, it is beginning to dawn on me that the man so emphatically claiming to be the lead guitarist from Aerosmith is – in fact – a friend of Bob's from back home. Unfortunately, I have no way of ascertaining for certain. I know nothing whatsoever about the band: their names, the titles of their albums, nothing. All of this poses an awkward moral dilemma. If he is, indeed, who he claims to be, then he'd be justifiably furious if some young upstart accuses him otherwise. Being the lead guitarist of Aerosmith for so many years must have been terribly hard work at times, and to have the very foundation of one's working life questioned in an S&M club in Prague at 3.00 a.m. by a twenty-seven-year-old stringer for *Kerrang!* would be the most savage of affronts.

Nonetheless, the journalists' code of conduct emphatically states that one must only publish celebrity interviews if the personality in question isn't, in fact, just somebody pretending. There was a notorious rumour in London, a few years ago, which alleged that a journalist called Henry Porter was offered an exclusive face-to-face interview with Meryl Streep ('She asked for you especially,' the PR had explained) only to discover weeks after its high-profile publication that his interviewee was, in fact, a nobody actress with long blonde hair. To this day he is referred to behind his back as Henry Streep-Porter. I'll be damned if I'm going to allow the same pitiable fate to befall me.

But, still, there's a return air fare at stake here, and Frank's answers are certainly passable – perhaps even more erudite than the real Frank Crowley's would be (assuming that my companion *isn't* the real Frank Crowley) so I conclude that, for now, I will keep my options open. At about this point Frank returns to the table.

'Where were we?'

'We were discussing the imminent bloody demise of the ruling classes.'

'Right. Well, as I was saying . . .' And so the night progresses.

———

I awake early to a sunny morning, so I decide to make a drive out of Prague and into the countryside. I have a notion to visit Terezin, a small fortified town on the road to Dresden, which was transformed into a concentration camp-cum-Nazi-PR-enterprise during the Second World War. Terezin's claim to notoriety was that the SS High Command commissioned a film to be shot there entitled *Hitler Builds A City For The Jews*, in which jolly, grinning Jews were seen playing rugby and swimming and putting on amateur dramatic productions for each other.

The movie was subsequently presented to any wartime humanitarian groups who wanted to know what the hell had happened to all the Jews – why there weren't any about any more – and, when they saw it, they were successfully placated. The ruse was an all-round triumph, and, milked of their PR-worth, the Terezin inmates were promptly shipped off to Auschwitz.

The drive towards Terezin is picturesque and charming: tiny, ancient rural villages where little old Czech ladies gather hay in the morning sun, grinning and waving at me. I wind down the window, turn off the radio, and allow the silence into the car.

Of course, these are the same villages (and the same silence) that thousands of Prague Jews also experienced on that final journey before being transformed into living, breath-

———

ing propaganda exercises, so I attempt to summon a suitably sombre mood for my outing.

I attempt to picture myself as one of those Jews. But its difficult. Every time I gaze at the trees and fields and ponder upon how little the landscape must have changed in fifty years, a recently erected building or billboard hoves into view. As much as I try to empathize, the billboards blow it for me.

————

I park the car on the outskirts of town next to a butcher's, the name of which – I ascertain after consulting my phrase book – is Pleased To Meat You (there's a lot of competition: sometimes the funny name swings it). And next to the butcher's, I see a tiny street. It isn't so much a street, it's far less than that: a crumpled synagogue, and a little wooden house next to it. And that's all.

There's a huge tree at the front of the street, next to the butcher's. If you are an engrossed-by-trees type (I am wholly ignorant about natural beauty: I could be right next to a Mighty Redwood and spend the whole time staring at the ground on insect-alert) then you may look at the tree, say 'wow' at how breathtaking it is, and not even notice the synagogue and the house. The tree is far more significant than what is behind it.

Even though the morning is turning cold, the owner of the house is in the front garden wearing a thin cotton dress, sweeping up the leaves. I glance at her – she is very old. The synagogue is very old too, paper thin, and the door is open. So I go inside to have a look.

There's a service going on, but only a handful of people are there to see it. I pick up a prayer book, and, not knowing Hebrew, read the English translation for a while.

Then I head back outside, and smile at the old lady, still sweeping up the leaves. I point at the little blue tattoo on her arm.

'Auschwitz?' I ask. She nods.

'I'm a Jew too,' I say.

'Oh,' replies the lady. And she carries on sweeping.

————

————

Terezin town centre is a slightly eerie and a slightly dull place. There is a big square, encircled by clipped trees, and the surrounding streets are shadowy, even though it is a sunny day. On the corner, the old school has been turned into a Holocaust museum, albeit an understated one. Unlike the Holocaust Museum in Washington DC, there are no gimmicks here.

In Washington, you can gaze through little slits in the wall and see old film of women being shot and bodies being piled. These peepshows are the most popular attraction of the Washington museum, and sometimes you have to wait ages to have a peep yourself.

Compared to that, the Terezin museum is positively archaic – just the odd glass cabinet housing childrens' drawings and old concentration camp outfits. There's a film showing in the corner on a little video, but it's a low budget affair: just interviews with Terezin survivors, and nowhere near as engaging as, say, *Schindler's List*, in which you get to see the lot. In fact, my journey to Terezin is panning out as an all-round less emotional experience than my visit to the Empire, Leicester Square for the opening night of the Spielberg movie.

Which is a shame. The whole point about this holiday was that it was to be the finest one anybody could hope for – and, in my book, fine holidays include becoming emotionally outraged about unthinkable tragedies. It's just that Spielberg shifted the goalposts, Holocaust-wise, and now it's difficult for everyone else to keep up. Big budgets and all.

———

As I drive out of Terezin, I think of my girlfriend back home, and I think of my grandmother. My grandmother once told me that, should I marry out of the faith, my wife would one day turn to me – maybe ten or fifteen years from now – and say, 'You're nothing but a dirty Jew.'

'That's the way it is with non-Jews,' my grandmother would say. 'That is what they really think of us.'

It was clear cut for my grandmother. She believed all non-Jews to be horned warriors of Satan, and she didn't want one in the family. I once told my non-Jewish girlfriend that story, and, thereafter, whenever I did something that annoyed her, she'd say, 'You dirty Jew,' and we'd both laugh. It was a running joke.

7

Back in the London again. I arrived at Gatwick early this morning in low spirits. Delta Air had forgotten to remind passengers that there would be a five-hour wait in Frankfurt, and somebody had patently forgotten to remind Frankfurt airport that passenger seating would be a pleasant bonus in the waiting area. Wholly without hard currency, I attempted to buy some magazines and cigarettes with my Visa card, but the old lady at the newspaper stand thought that this was the funniest notion she'd ever come across in her life, and, chuckling to herself, proceeded to vociferously point me out to every other customer in the store.

'DER JÜDE WILL EINE KREDIT KARTE,' she hollered (Germans are the one race who can yell and chuckle simultaneously), 'UND WIR MÜSSEN IHN UND SEINE MEN-SCHEN VERNICHTEN.' And everyone laughed.

'If I'd known you wanted some evening entertainment I'd have worn a funny hat, you grizzled old Nazi hag,' I muttered to myself, walked out into the concourse, and sat on my coat like a hippie for four hours.

————

So, I'm back in London with a day to kill before the QE2 sets sail for New York. To prepare myself for the onslaught of showbiz pulchritude I am evidently about to encounter in New York, and in order to practise being appropriately lowly in the presence of excellence, I resolve to pass time by stopping off at this morning's celebrity launch of the annual breast cancer charity jamboree, Trading Places.

Let me explain the concept. Trading Places is an amusing charity initiative in which famous, beguiling people like Marie Helvin and Richard Branson pretend to be normal for the day! And it's not just celebrities! Secretaries get to pretend to be managers! Butlers pretend they are aristocracy! And so on. Today – for one day only – divides will be bridged, paupers will pretend to be moneyed, and fantastically glamorous show business figures will pretend to be lowly nobodies who work in banks. The glitzy showbiz launch is at the Queen's Theatre in the West End, and it promises to be the most star-studded of mornings.

On my arrival in the foyer, I am immediately seized by charity worker Sian, who explains the itinerary to me.

'Well,' she says, 'we've got some celebrity guests, a slide show, drinks, and a few surprises too!'

She briskly hands me over to Stephen, who is to be my own special charity-worker for the morning, and he takes me into the auditorium.

'It's such an innovative charity concept,' I say, hoping for some form of rapport with my new friend, 'that it almost gives people a reason to have breast cancer.'

At this, Stephen goes silent on me, looks at the floor, and I make a mental note, in future, to go easier on the praise.

The moment I walk through the door of the auditorium, TV agony aunt Claire Rayner, dressed in a maid's outfit and masquerading as a humble waitress, thrusts a drink into my hand, while the sound system blasts out lyrically appropriate songs such as 'The Great Pretender', 'Changes', and – struggling somewhat – 'Walk Like An Egyptian' and 'Like A Virgin'. While we wait for the show to begin, ex-catwalk beauty Marie Helvin, pretending to be a common, servile usherette, walks up and down the aisles throwing sweets to a large group of (authentic, not pretending) semi-deaf orphan children who have been bussed in to add some pathos to the morning. (Maybe all the breast cancer sufferers were busy.) Then the lights go out, and, with a small hum of enchantment, Cilla Black appears on the stage.

–––––

'We're going to have a lorra lorra laughs today,' she announces.

Everyone cheers, the semi-deaf orphans, the paparazzi, everyone.

'But,' she adds seriously, 'let's not forget about breast cancer.'

Everyone nods solemnly, and we are shown a brief slide show of yellow, festering, ulcerating cells.

–––––

'Taraaa,' says Cilla, and everybody claps.

——

Back in the theatre bar, I get chatting to TV meteorologist Bill Giles' agent – a young man called Carli – about his client's current celebrity tour of comedy clubs around Britain.

'I don't see Bill as just a weatherman,' he portends, enthusiastically. 'I see him as a solo entertainer.' He happily, and almost apologetically, wipes away the potato salad that I dropped on his suede loafers, and continues. 'I don't see Bill in a suit. I see him in shorts and a bermuda shirt. I see him more . . .' Carli pauses momentarily, 'showbiz.'

Carli has only been with Bill for three months, but he's already discovered the beauty of meteorology. 'I never used to think twice about the weather, but now I never miss a broadcast. I think it's wonderful.'

Then, suddenly, Bill himself approaches the table. Carli introduces me, and the three of us stand around in a slightly awkward silence.

'Ahh,' says Carli. 'Mmm. Yes.'

'So, Bill,' I begin after a moment. 'Do you prefer centigrade to Fahrenheit?'

'I'm definitely a centigrade man,' Bill replies. 'What about you?'

'I prefer Fahrenheit.'

'Oh really?' contends Bill. 'Most youngsters go for centigrade.'

'Perhaps so,' I say. 'But not me.'

We drift off into an awkward silence again, so Bill excuses himself and rushes away.

'Tell me about Bill's comedy act,' I say to Carli.

'I can do better than that,' he replies. 'Why don't you come to the show tonight? We're doing a warm-up down the road in Hayes.'

'But I've got to get across to Southampton for the QE2. I'm off to New York tomorrow.'

'Well, that's absolutely no problem at all. Hayes is on the way. Come along. You'll have the most wonderful time.'

——

——

So I do. The Beck Theatre in Hayes stands a stone's throw from Hayes Footcare and Hayes Funerals, and is, Carli informs me, just down the road from Seers Green, the Sunset Strip of the Beaconsfield area, where Bill lives. Sharing this neighbourhood are, amongst others, Val Doonican, Cilla Black, the Bee Gees, and, by one of those remarkable coincidences, Ian McCaskill.

I arrive as the audience is filtering in – perhaps twenty-five in total – and, just as I am about to take my seat, Carli approaches nervously.

'Jon,' he says. 'Glad you could come. There are more than twenty-five people here, aren't there?'

'Yes, definitely,' I reply. The lights go down.

'Give him a big clap,' whispers Carli, as Bill appears swaggering on the stage. We roar our appreciation, and the now thirty-strong audience joins in with an almost religious fervour.

'I'm here to talk about the funny side of weather,' begins Bill. 'If you pay attention, I'm sure you'll learn more than Michael Fish knows.'

There is a huge laugh, especially from Carli, and animated clapping.

'One of the reasons why a depression is called a depression is because it gives you very depressing weather!'

More loud laughter and clapping.

'He's really animated tonight,' whispers Carli between shrieks. 'They love it.' And they do. 'If you think *this* is good, you should have seen the Robin Hood Theatre in Nottingham. It was *euphoric*.'

One and a half hours later, and it's time for the question-and-answer session. A sea of hands rise, and Bill points to a man in a red sweater waving frantically.

'Why is the weather only a minute long?' asks the man. 'Why is it over so quickly?'

'I tell you, I fight tooth and nail for more time,' replies Bill. 'Next?'

And Bill fends off questions with the natural ease of an aged schoolteacher or an established superstar – which he is – as he tells me later.

'I can't go anywhere without being recognized,' he says. 'I was swimming in Nairobi and an Indian man was sitting on the edge of the pool. He was so surprised to see me that he actually fell in. It's horrible for the family, but I enjoy it.'

To what does he attribute his success?

'I'm hungry. You've got to be hungry to do it,' he replies confidently, looking down at his BBC weatherman's tie covered in very small cloud symbols. 'I'm the best.'

It's getting late, so I say my goodbyes. On the way out, I spot Carli, grinning a victorious grin. 'He's so talented,' he smiles. 'He's so much better than Fish and McCaskill. I want to get him into rehearsals. Imagine how good he'll be then. After rehearsals. Imagine that.'

————

I've booked myself a night at the Holiday Inn in Southampton: the ship leaves early tomorrow morning, and, as I walk to my car, I notice a weather-beaten young man clutching an autograph book near the stage door. I ask him how he's doing.

'I've only had one since Monday, but it was a good one – Wayne Dobson.'

'Who?'

He looks at me with horror. 'Wayne *Dobson*. He works with Joe Longthorne. He's a magician. Famous.' I attempt to conceal my ignorance, and fail. He leaps to Mr Dobson's defence.

'He's not just a magician, you know. He's a comedy impressionist as well.'

He pulls out his autograph book, flicks past Nanette Newman and Ray Gosling ('He was in *Gosling's Travels*. He told me he wasn't famous, but I knew he was'), and finds Wayne Dobson.

'To John,' it says. 'Regards, Wayne Dobson.' John smiles. 'They all call me John. They all know my name. They're all very nice. Well. Not all. John Quentin out of *Return Of The Antelope*. He was rude. He threatened to call security, said I was tormenting him. But I got him in the end. Look.' John shows me his book. 'To John,' it says. 'Regards, John Quentin.'

John pauses thoughtfully. 'No, I wasn't too keen on that

————

John Quentin, but Cilla Black was nice. She called me "Ducky".'

———

A few years ago, John tells me, he attempted to give up his ever-increasing obsession.

'I went to Yorkshire on holiday. Stayed there for two years. I just ran and swam all day. It did me the world of good. It was wonderful. And then it all went wrong.' He shivers at the memory.

'I was shopping in Doncaster, just walking around, minding my own business. And I looked behind me. If only I hadn't looked behind me.' He pauses, sighs, and continues.

'So I looked behind me, and Kevin Cawley out of *Albion Market* was there, walking into the Dome. And it all came flooding back. So I came back to Hayes. I've been here ever since.'

He looks around the car park, and then back at me. 'It's not a bad life. Meeting Cilla Black was good. She called me "Ducky". I like that. Famous people are important. They're better than me with the spotlight shining on them. Famous people . . .'

He struggles for an explanation. 'Famous people can go to the police and ask for protection, and they'll get it, just like that.'

He clicks his fingers.

'Just like that.'

He goes silent on me now, so I gaze up at the sky. Dark clouds are beginning to form, sweeping across the theatre, casting an ominous shadow over the car park. They could be isobars. But maybe it's just post-gig euphoria.

———

While all this was happening – it transpires – Cunard had sent word to the QE2 that I was to be offered all the finest treatment for the duration of my five-day voyage to New York. Just a few years ago, the ship hit a rock near Martha's Vineyard, and the news has just been reported that P&O Ferries are planning an even more outstandingly flamboyant vessel

———

to rival Cunard's jewel. Consequently, favourable publicity is uppermost in everybody's mind, and from the moment I board the ship in Southampton I find myself being fussed over like an invalid child or a glamorous VIP.

I'm invited to meet the Captain and the Chief Purser and the Cruise Manager. I'm fed all the canapés any man could ask for. I am wooed onto the stage in the Grand Lounge to start the Daily Horse Race. (Wood horses/a big dice/six lovely ladies).

'Giddy-up,' I say. 'And they're off.'

———

I am in hell. Admittedly, I've not picked a great time for transatlantic sailing if I want to have fun and make new friends. By unfortunate coincidence, I'm a passenger on their worst-attended – and roughest – cruise for years. This is the Marie Celeste. The force of the waves are vigorous enough to knock you out of bed. The moment the water hits the port-hole, it freezes and forms huge icicles, which are swept away and replaced by the next bombardment.

This is, in fact, *worse* than the Marie Celeste, because the Marie Celeste didn't offer Carnival Magic's Showtime Big Band Sound and a celebrity guest lecture by TV astrologer Russell Grant as the week's highlights. This is the Marie Celeste with Russ Abbott at the helm. This is 'Sunday Night At The Marie Celeste Palladium'.

It wasn't always this way, one assumes. But some fool twenty-five years ago must have decided that swish deco was old hat and late-sixties tack was the elegant way forward, and consequently, the vast majority of the ship's interior looks like the set of the *Banana Splits*. The disco bar is straight out of *Saturday Night Fever*, the overall ambience (besides the wholly isolated Class A fake thirties swank corridor) is Butlins with portholes.

I have been located in a Grade D cabin, which is large, but not ostentatious. The cabins here range from Class A to Class M, and from $3000 to $100 per person, per night. The $3000 cabins have their own private bit of deck, a personal butler, a TV the size of my flat. The $100 cabins are straight

out of the *Caine Mutiny*. They are underwater. You have to
row. The view is shite.

They don't call them 'cabins', by the way. They call them
'Staterooms'. This, one can only assume, is so that pensioners
from Peckham who've spent their lives saving up for a meagre
five-day trip in Grade Z can go home and tell their neighbours
that they were put in the most charming Stateroom, which
happened to be the same size as their fridge-freezer, but it
didn't matter because it was a Stateroom, and that's what the
Queen sleeps in.

Every morning, the Captain delivers his address to the
ship, which consists of variations on the following: 'Well, I've
been Captain for forty years now, and I've never experienced
such a thrillingly hazardous sea. Goodness, it must be exciting
for you to be on such a rocky journey, rather than the usual
stuffy old peachy sunshine we've come to expect here on the
QE2. Now you can go home and tell your friends that you
were on the most tumultuous crossing that *this* Captain has
ever encountered. And *that's* official. By the way, don't forget
Freddie 'Parrot Face' Davies' guest lecture in the Grand
Lounge tonight. That's Freddie 'Parrot Face' Davies, with dancing by the Cunard Cuties, six lovely ladies with legs to match
– Grand Lounge, 8.00 p.m. Bon voyage!'

Due to the hurricane, the pools have been emptied, the
health spa and gymnasium are closed, and many of the in-
ship movies are cancelled. Consequently, the staff, remaining
admirably unwavering throughout the entire Big Wave Crisis,
put on a splendidly ad hoc substitute social itinerary of 'scarf
folding for beginners', 'seaweed as beauty tip' (there are many
fabulous things you can do with seaweed, besides draping it
all over your face and scaring your sister) and 'scarf folding
(advanced)' for those who attended the first course and want
to delve deeper into this complex and multifarious pastime.

'There now,' says the folding instructor. 'You won't let
your husband down with a knot like that.'

'I didn't know there were so many ways to tie a knot
in a scarf,' I say to the woman after the performance (the
demonstrations always end with an informal discussion
group). 'But now the weights have been lifted from my eyes.'

'There are many ways,' she replies. 'There is a knot for every occasion.'

'They really *are* excellent,' adds Russell Grant, sitting on the next table. 'I'll have to try it myself. Ha ha! Ha ha ha!'

'Ha ha,' adds his manager, sitting on the next seat.

'Thank you very much,' replies the teacher. And she adds, 'High praise indeed.'

'So,' I ask Russell. 'You're giving a lecture?'

'Yes, yes,' he replies. 'I gave one on the ship a few years ago and it was hugely successful, so they've asked me back. You really should come, you know. Learn something about yourself. Eh? Eh? Hey hey hey!'

'So are you just giving the lecture and then flying back to England?'

'No, ha ha ha,' he replies. 'Oh no no.'

'Ha ha ha,' agrees his manager. 'No no no. Don't be so silly.'

'Oh no no,' continues Russell. 'I wouldn't waste my time with *that*.'

'No, Russell is going to see Twentieth Century Fox because they've got a *really big* series idea they want to put his way. They really are *very open* to comedy astrology. It's the latest thing.'

'I'm really *very big* in America,' continues Russell. 'It's embarrassing really.'

'Tell me,' I say. 'I've always wanted to ask an astrologer this question.'

'Oh yes?' says Russell.

'You don't totally believe everything you say, do you?'

'What do you mean?'

'All that, "Money worries on Tuesday" stuff. You don't *really* believe it?'

'Listen here, young man,' snaps Russell, giving me an angry glare, 'I take great offence to that, and if you want to make more of it then you can speak to my lawyer back in England. Okay? OKAY?'

And, furiously, he and his manager stand and walk away. I debate running after them to apologize, but my attention is distracted by the introduction of an informal lecture/therapy session from one of the passengers entitled, 'Do It!', which she begins by informing us that if we successfully Did It, we will be far more capable in every aspect of our lives.

After ten minutes, I still can't quite work out what It is, which is a shame because – after the Russell Grant experience – I am desperately in need of some capableness, and it is indisputable that the speaker is massively, formidably capable and has obviously done It in spades, whatever It is.

Unfortunately she is also an appalling person (brash, loud, Californian) and consequently a lousy advertisement, which is why I am only half listening. The whole thing is rather like going to a seminar on leading a full and happy life hosted by Sylvia Plath. I don't know. If this is how you turn out once you've Done It, then pass the sad-tablets. The text of the seminar, I believe, is to love yourself, forgive yourself, blame yourself, build a shell around yourself, bury those pesky feelings, bury them deep, deep down. (Tick tick tick. Boom! Ted Bundy.)

'I'm just a faciliator,' explains the lady. 'But I'm giving you *permission* to like yourself today.' Well, gee, thanks.

Beside Russell, his manager, me and the capable lady, there are about four other passengers on board this crossing, including Philip from Manchester who is very, very big indeed in locker room units, and, on the afternoon of the second day, insists on showing me his company's brochure.

'You've got to admit,' he says, pointing at a photograph of a wooden thing, 'it's a welcome addition to any locker room facility. Just look at the tits on that.'

I study the photo, wondering, goofily, which segment is classed at the 'tit'.

'No,' tuts Philip, pointing at a passing waitress, 'her.' I dutifully survey her breasts, making 'mmm'-type noises, and we lapse into a long silence, broken only by the two of us being flung across the dance floor and smashed against the Harrods window display by a particularly thrilling gust of wind.

––––

Suppertime on the QE2 is the one aspect of on-board life

––––

which is just as flamboyant as one imagines, and I order the seafood salad, which arrives looking like a David Attenborough documentary with tossed lettuce. There are shellfish here that people go to museums to look at, shellfish that people gaze at and say, 'Wow. Jesus.'

Our waiter, Simon, is a remarkable man, gliding through the restaurant, exuding a dignity and poise that embodies all that the QE2 must once have been.

He used to work at Buckingham Palace as an underbutler, and after a few nights' dinners, he begins coyly to recount tales of state banquets and small pleasantries that members of the Royal Family once uttered to him.

He remembers the day that the Queen remarked upon how clean the silver was. And when he remembers this, his face breaks out into a broad smile.

'I could write a book,' he says, 'about all the things that have happened to me.'

'You should,' I reply.

'Now's the time for me to write a book,' he continues. 'They say that the time to write a book is when everything is finished, and there's nothing more left to happen.'

'That's what they say,' I agree.

'I worked for the Queen fifteen years ago,' he says, 'before everything went wrong.'

'It's a terrible shame,' I reply. 'But time marches on, and things change.'

'Yes,' he says. 'My wife was a wonderful woman.'

After supper, on my way back to the cabin, I gaze into the old photographs on the wall of the Piano Bar, reminders of the days when transatlantic travel was all the fashionable rage. Photos of past celebrity passengers: Cary Grant (ah! From Cary Grant to Russell Grant in only forty years), David Niven and Marilyn Maxwell adorn the walls of the bar.

And as I look into the photographs – Walt Disney and his family grinning over champagne in the First Class Restaurant, Marilyn Maxwell perched excitedly on the ship's railings, gazing into New York Harbour, her skirt blowing in the wind – as I gaze upon these photos I realize that the experience of sliding slowly across the Atlantic towards the mysterious, sophisticated New World must once have been extraordinary. But this is the nineties, and the minute we disembark, I'm convinced that we'll be immediately killed by a street gang of crack addicts.

8

My suspicion of New York stems, in part, from a week's holiday I had here with my mother's mother many years ago, when I was just a kid. My grandfather was off on one of his mysterious business trips (they never told me what he did, and when I pressed them, would reluctantly and enigmatically reply 'imports and exports', and swiftly change the subject. Until I was twelve, I was convinced that he was an arms dealer. Then I found out: kitchen utensils. I'd read the signs wrong – I'd been mistaking humiliation for intrigue).

So my grandmother decided that the two of us must bond, and took me to New York for a holiday. Why she chose New York, I'll never understand; she suffered from a nervous disposition, and would clutch her heart every time the phone rang. So from the minute we got off the plane, she was convinced we'd entered a war zone.

'We can't go on the subway,' she'd yell. 'We'll be killed. Don't touch that dog – it may have rabies. Don't talk to *anyone*. Just don't *talk*,' she'd scream. 'They hate the British. Don't buy *any drinks*. They may be *spiked with heroin*.' And so on.

My grandmother, it transpires, turned out to be right after all. Since crack hit New York big, and turned everyone who sniffed it into the Bosnian Serbs, the city has become intolerable. I disembarked three hours ago and I've already met a vagrant who, just ten minutes before, was beaten half to death with a length of pipe by a group of twelve-year-old boys (I ask him if he needs any help: he replies that he would like a cigarette).

'The worst thing about it,' he says, wiping the blood from his eyes, and puffing heavily, 'is that it happened today.'

And what day is it today, as if it really matters? It is his birthday.

I beg to contend: there is something more appalling than being savaged within an inch of your life on a day that apportions your beating an ironic resonance, and that is to be battered by a bunch of hoodlums who were born after Wham! were big. I don't know about you, but if I'm going to be murdered by a crazed gang of thugs, I want the swine to – at least – have pubic hair. Where's the fun in becoming an adult, when children start punishing your inadequacies? The joke going around New York now is that the criminals are so young that they don't have drive-by shootings, they have cycle-by shootings.

But I'm not here to celebrate New York's lurid heritage. My wealthy showbiz-agent cousin Joel has paid for me to stay for one night at the ultra-exclusive Phillipe Starck-designed Royalton Hotel. And – yes – for all the weary cynicism, I am pitiably awed.

'Wow,' I say, as I walk into the fabulously sleek sushi-restaurant-esque lobby (the door was opened for me by four hugely attractive Official Filipino Door Openers, calling me 'Sir'. Of course, I had absolutely no idea how to respond. I'm pathetically grateful to find a chocolate on my pillow last thing at night, so to have a group of Filipinos being humble and lowly makes me want to die with joy. I am in bigot heaven). Uncommon beauty is a job prerequisite, it seems, like we're schmuck enough to order more food if the waitress looks like Kate Moss. Okay – fuck it – it works. If you are an uncontrollably lascivious anorexic, take a tip: stay elsewhere.

'Wow,' I say, as I mistake the wall for an elevator, and spend ten minutes wondering what the hell is taking it so long (everything is very dark and integrated).

'Wow,' I say, as I fall off the aesthetically terrific but lamentably three-legged Philippe Starck chair and pour a cup of $4 post-deco coffee all over my trousers. (There *are* drawbacks – I was in the toilet for twenty minutes before I worked out which bit to urinate against).

Even the in-house porno movies have elegant, stylish titles: *Majestic Dawn Knight*, *Luncheon With Amber Lyn*, *Taboo IX*, and so on. *Lesbian Lavatory Lust* this is not. Unfortunately. The other little filth-fest complication is that the movies have to be ordered and brought to your room, and I'm very old-fashioned about this. The thought of some exquisitely refined bedroom attendant knocking on my door and saying: 'Here's your copy of *Zen Flower Fistfuck*,' sends shivers down my spine.

I'm sure he wouldn't – but imagine if he *did* – point and laugh and call me 'Mr Can't Get A Lay'. This can scar a man for life.

I opt, eventually, for the assiduously educational (as they say) *Kama Sutra*, and manage about two-and-a-half minutes, during which an Aryan couple shag each other against a tree while the commentary announces: 'And this is called "The Forest". His arrow, tipped with lotus flowers, strikes love into her sweet, sugar cane bow strung with humming bees.' Believe me, it's hard to beat off when you're confronted by commentary like this. Take a tip – turn the sound down.

As I wait for the arrival of my exciting showbiz cousin, I bide away the time by pacing the room, trying to cover every square inch of the carpet, trying to get what my money's worth would be, had I been paying. I watch all thirty-one channels on the TV, my personal favourite being the twenty-four-hour weather channel. ('It's a little bit misty in Minneapolis today, so we sent Bob down to have a look. Hey Bob. Hey Joe. It sure is misty, and I've got Suzanne, our Mist Correspondent with me here. Hey Suzanne. Hey Bob. This is some mist.') I think: how wonderful, how comfortingly banal. Now it's been proven categorically that TV violence is responsible for all of society's ills, twenty-four hours of weather per day can only be a step back to basics. Is it too much to surmise, my thoughts continue, that if every channel were a weather channel, crime statistics would plummet and everyone would know in advance when to wear a coat?

But then the news flashes that there's a terrifying hurricane in Iowa killing all the farmers and decimating all the crops, and the mood turns evil. The presenters are thrilled. It is startling, and somewhat chilling, to witness such ill-disguised glee amongst so much chaos and mayhem and death. They can hardly conceal their giggles.

I switch off in disgust, feeling an inherent mistrust of the twenty-four-hour weather folk, being, undoubtedly, enemies of Mother Earth, the one group of people who are secretly ebullient about impending ozone doom, furtively spraying cans of anti-perspirant deodorant in the air when nobody's looking. So, with sorrowful meditation, I hit the bar.

The thing about the Royalton, and the reason why Joel patronizes the place so often, is this: every lunchtime, the main power players of the New York magazine and music industries meet here and – as the saying goes – make and break careers. Tina Brown (*The New Yorker*), Pete Townshend, and on and on. Joel networks.

The restaurant is separated into three easily recognizable Power Areas, each defined by the colour of the chairs. White, Blue and Green. Pete and Tina and the other marvellous eaters get to sit in Green. If you edit *Vogue* or *Vanity Fair* or *Cosmo*, you get Green. If you assistant-edit *The Village Voice* or *Spin*, you get Blue. If you work for *Shoe And Leather News* or *Whales and Whaling Monthly*, or *Which Droplet* you get White. If they put you in White, you may as well buy yourself a hoover and sweep yourself up.

I am, therefore, hoping beyond hope that Joel gets Green too, for that would surely make him the only Ronson in the history of the clan to be eligible for Green. Here I am, all these years later, still attempting – with pathetic eagerness – to unearth some intrigue, somewhere.

To tell you the truth, I'm downplaying my family's prestigious ancestry somewhat. Just last week, a distant cousin – who we'd never heard of – approached my mother as part of her research for the Ronson family tree. It transpires, she told my mother, that we Ronsons were so proud to be Ronsons back in days of olde – that being a Ronson was such an excellently exclusive thing to be – that we couldn't bear to copulate with non-Ronsons. So Ronsons have been marrying Ronsons for generations. Thanks, guys. With that sort of genetic explosion going on inside me, no wonder my hairline's receding.

But when Joel finally walks through the door, I say 'Wow' one more time, for Green showers out of his every pore. He's an imposing figure: looks just about as un-Ronson as one can get. A foot taller than me, fastidiously dressed – okay: it's never been proven that there's an inalienable link between genetics and where you shop, but I'm always reading of identical twins who were separated at birth and ended up buying the same waistcoat. Wealth and success has brought him good looks.

As he walks towards my table, grinning a broad grin, the elevator door opens, and Pete Townshend walks out into the lobby. And as I watch, Joel, as elegantly as a swan, spins round, clasps him by the hand, and says, 'Hi, Pete. Joel Ronson. I'm a BIG fan.' 'Hi, yeah, great,' says Townshend, and then it is over. Joel sails through the lobby towards my table, extends his hand, and says, 'Hi Jon. Hope you're having a good stay.'

We are put in White. Joel is crestfallen, but hides it well.

'Now,' he says, 'they have to come to me.'

We're about four miles away from Calvin Klein, Bianca Jagger, David Geffen and Jann Wenner (*Rolling Stone*) in the cheap seats, our death throes accompanied by the music of a million chirping mobile phones. Media moguls from across Manhattan have emerged to find themselves in the same restaurant, and they're *still* calling each other from adjacent tables, I swear to God. I guess that when they finally meet up, they fax each other small talk.

They screech into their mobiles, telling LA 'no', holding Tokyo.

'Okay,' reply their secretaries from the next seat. And in Tokyo, one assumes, everybody stops what they're doing, and just stands there. Lunch is dull, Joel mumbles, disinterested, glancing constantly towards where the grass – and chairs – are Greener. But he is a Ronson, and that is the way things go. We are doomed to White for life.

––––

Anyway, to cut a long story short, Joel has this boy – smooth, like Tony Orlando, songs and jokes – who's playing this weekend in a little club in Las Vegas. A classy affair with attractive dancers and a comedian who tells observation gags ('Don't you hate it when you go to the toilet and there's no toilet paper!' That sort of thing). Joel's boy is heading the bill, and if I promise to put his act in the book, Joel will pay my ticket to Vegas. I gladly agree.

The trip will take place in three days, so I make a plan to

while away the time at the movies. But the bastard audiences insist, *ad infinitum*, on shouting warnings as loudly as possible to the various screen characters at key plot moments. Thus: *Alien 3* ('There's one big motherfucking alien round the corner, Ripley. I wouldn't go round there if I were you'), *Total Recall* ('Your wife's a motherfucking bitch, don't trust her'), *The Piano* ('The instrument is simply a metaphor for her spiritual essence. If you take it away from her, she'll be left an empty shell. You motherfucker'). And so on.

New York's cinemas, like London's, have a dreadful policy of insisting you sit in your allocated, numbered seat, and, like London, the ticket sellers have devised a little amusement for themselves entitled 'Put Jon Next To The Man With Nasal Difficulties'. After a while I can stand it no longer, so I hit the streets.

There's a saying that New York isn't Mecca – it just smells like it – and it's something of a shock to be back in reality, back in the land beyond the Royalton, where the only people willing to be nice to me are the Krishnas. I'm a stranger in a strange town: I wander aimlessly through Chinatown, down to the Financial District, and up into East Village. New York screams and yells and billows, so I take sanctuary in a tourist information centre somewhere in the muggy, dank airless Hell they call Midtown.

'What the *hell* do you *want*?' screams the woman behind the desk. 'Get out of my office *now* or I'll have you *shot*.'

These aren't, admittedly, her words verbatim, but she possesses an extraordinary talent of being able to say, 'Can I help you?' and make it sound like she's just threatened to set an organized crime syndicate on me.

'I'm alone in New York for the afternoon and I was wondering if you could give me some advice on what to do,' I reply.

'What in *God's* name are you asking *me* for, turd breath?' she yells. Sort of. The actual words that come out of her mouth are, 'Have you been to the top of the Empire State Building?' But it is much the same thing.

'I did on a previous visit,' I say. 'What else is there to do?'

'Oh, take this and fuck off,' she replies, hurling a brochure on New York's guided walks in my direction. I thank her, leave the office, and sit down for a coffee to read the brochure.

This, under the circumstances, turns out to be rather tricky. The coffee bar, like many of Manhattan's interiors, has an air-conditioning system equipped with the kinetic power to pick you up, spin you around, and dump you in a strange new land where brightly coloured dwarfs gather around you singing 'Ding Dong The Witch Is Dead'. New York's huddled masses may be yearning to breathe free, but that's no reason to blast them into space with enough recycled oxygen to make Jupiter inhabitable.

I decide against ordering the Coffee Of The Month ('This Month – Brazilian'), as a symbolic stance against the heinous international trend of perpetually redefining products and hoping that we the consumer are schmuck enough not to notice. It was bad enough when British Rail started doing it with their sandwiches: ('Sandwich Of The Month. This month – Cheese!') and I'm damned if I'm going to succumb to this cunning corporate sham while on holiday. So instead, I ask the waitress what last month's Coffee Of The Month was.

'Brazilian,' she replies haughtily, throwing me a 'Come-And-Have-A-Go-If-You-Think-You're-Hard-Enough' look.

'I'll take the Brazilian,' I reply, sheepishly, and, defying the gales, bury myself in the brochure to peruse the walks on offer.

To be totally frank, I've always laboured under the impression that guided walks were an archaic concept, trampled wholly by the magnificent boot of technological excellence. 'Geological Walks Of New York' takes, for instance, about one-and-a-half hours by foot, and I reckon I could do it in my Rover 216S in about four minutes. (Believe me, you can derive far more pleasure from identifying granite if you are doing it from the driver's seat of a speeding 1.6.)

Indeed, my parents were sticklers for all things guided, and would constantly be taking my brother and I on surprise organized weekend walking trips around London.

'We're going to see "Historic Barts and Smithfield" today,' my dad would yell after we had passed the Severn Bridge, the point of no return. I'd fall back into my seat with horror, a plethora of vital questions racing through my mind. Questions like:

1. What the hell is a 'bart'?
2. If I did ascertain what a 'bart' was, why the hell would I want to go and look at one, historic or otherwise?
3. What possible thrill could I derive from spending an afternoon with somebody who considers bart-spotting to be a special delight; a person who might exclaim, 'Why, what an astonishing bart, dear'?

So my parents, my brother, me, eleven old ladies from South Carolina, and one strange, sweaty little man with a notebook would wander through the back streets of the East End, going 'mmmm'.

'This is Aldgate,' our tour guide would announce. 'So called because there used to be a gate here. Ald*gate*, you see. Fascinating really.' Everyone would look at Aldgate.

'This is Bishopsgate,' he'd continue, struggling somewhat. 'There used to be a gate here too. Bishops*gate* you see. Remarkable, really.'

Everyone would look at Bishopsgate. It would continue. These occasions were, of course, screamingly, mind-numbingly dull, but our guide would, nonetheless, divulge facts with a remarkable enthusiasm, especially when bearing in mind the preternatural dullness of the subject-matter. You could imagine him at home, discovering for the first time that fridge is short for refrigerator, and being completely blown away by the experience.

I remember, also, being taken on a walk called 'Sherlock Holmes' London', which was dreadful for all the obvious reasons – plus the added surprise reason that we didn't even make it to Baker Street, which you'd have thought was a must, really. I still shudder to recall just how frequently a single tour guide could announce, in the space of a single afternoon, '. . . and Holmes could deduce all this just by looking at him.'

We knew. Oh God, we knew.

So, my parents, my brother, me, fourteen fascinated Swedes, and the same strange, sweaty little man with a notebook would wander through the back streets of Covent Garden while our guide insisted on recounting the narrative of *The Blue Carbuncle* in its entirety, sub-plots, idioscyncracies, nuances and all. The Swedes would nod, fascinated, which did little to bolster my enthusiasm, did little to make me believe that I was actually missing something. When you come from Sweden, a tour of London's shrubbery would be a rare delight.

And after fifteen minutes of his words dissolving into a babbling nothingness, the guide would turn to me and say, rather startlingly, 'And you can guess which goose had gone, can't you?'

'Yes,' I'd reply. 'Ha ha ha.'

'And there,' he'd conclude, twinkling, 'is another mystery that the great sleuth actually solved.'

Yes, guided walks were the bane of my childhood, but here I am in New York with time to kill, and one must keep an open mind in all things. So, armed with my brochure, 'FUCKING HORRENDOUS WAYS TO SPEND AN AFTER-NOON IN THE BIG APPLE', I set off to discover this historic city's fascinating hidden gems.

I debate chancing my luck with 'Secret New York', but am put off by the title. Surely 'Secret New York' is only a secret because nobody can be fucked to go there. It stands to reason. If it wasn't shite, some nifty developer would have turned it into condos by now. One simply cannot keep entire regions of New York a secret. Somebody would tell.

———

Instead, I opt for 'Chic New York', a tour that promises to escort us peasant paupers to 'all of Manhattan's fanciest hot-spots', and the famous Dakota Building, 'the exact location where John Lennon of the Beatles was shot'.

Which is where the tour begins. The stores around Central Park West have the appearance of one gigantic garishly over-priced airport duty free shop, kind of like Geneva without the fondue, and this is where we wander. We photograph the outside of the Dakota Building, we photograph passing limos, we photograph large Fabergé eggs and expensive Cartier watches.

The tour ends with afternoon tea at the Waldorf Astoria,

———

a hotel which – in these recession-sodden days of consumer-led recreation – still knows how to make a customer feel like a piece of shit. These are waiters specialized in sniffing out a peasant fraud at a hundred paces, waiters who have trained at the HRH Princess Michael Of Kent Institute For Haughty Behaviour. This is a curious double-bluff, because at least seventy per cent of the clientele here are peasant frauds: Mr and Mrs Lower Middle Class from Hell who had triumphed in the 'Win A Night At The Waldorf Astoria By Completing The Following Sentence' contest in the *New Jersey Advertiser* ('I want to pretend to be moneyed for an evening because . . .').

In the bar, gentlemen in toupées that scream out the words 'middle management' pontificate wildly towards Middle-Eastern beauties who scream out the words 'high-class hooker'. One sweating fifty-year-old is fondling a stunning teenager with one hand, and posturing so recklessly with the other that, if he says anything even slightly more fascinating, he is certain to knock over a pot plant.

I had experienced this odd spectacle on the QE2: a theme-park jet set populated by people in polyester, where elegance is artifice, where high society cornucopia is as authentic as Eurodisney. I'm certain that an old-style high life does still thrive somewhere. Indeed, in Africa I had witnessed something resembling opulent gung-ho hedonism, albeit a beast teetering precariously on the verge of extinction. And, similarly, the Waldorf Astoria is a drab approximation of its former glory that appears to exist almost solely for the purposes of these guided tours.

But for all the causes deserving of abuse, the man that the waiters have elected to be most huffy towards today is me. The more the fuckers try and stop my fun, by snorting and tutting, the more my tenacity to be delighted at all costs is driving me onwards. I was hoping to while away my evening at the hotel, but the restaurant demands many days notice, and the big band dinner dance are all sold out. So there's nowhere in the entire hotel for me to sit and drink cocktails and nibble canapés.

'A warm welcome awaits you,' said the brochure. And the receptionist is trying, God bless her.

'You're welcome to stand in the foyer,' she says. 'I can certainly offer you the authorization to do that.'

'I must *drink*,' I yell. 'I must find a place to *drink* in.'

'We can certainly offer you the wine list so you can peruse our entire repertoire,' she replies.

'*Repertoire*?' I scream. 'What the *hell* are you talking about? I must *drink* and dance cheek to cheek.'

I miss the authentic yelling and the sirens of Midtown. I miss the Italians and the Puerto Ricans sauntering down decaying back alleys in immaculately choreographed dance routines. (That really does happen, you know. *West Side Story*'s urban authenticity has been criminally underrated: of course, apart from the scene where the guy roams through the Italian district yelling 'Maria! Maria!' Believe me, it is impossible to do that without three hundred ladies leaning out of their windows shouting: 'Yeah? What?')

While waiting for the connecting flight to the west coast, I check in to the incredibly run-down cockroach doom of the Chelsea Hotel, where Sid killed Nancy, where Edie Sedgwick set fire to herself, where Arthur C Clarke wrote *2001* and where Arthur Miller lived when he split up with Marilyn Monroe. I'm put in room 515, the very room in which Leonard Cohen had famous sex with Janice Joplin:

'I remember you well, at the Chelsea Hotel

Talking so loud and so sweet.

Giving me head on an unmade bed

While the limousines wait in the street'.

To maintain the historic authenticity, the hotel's managers appear to have opted not to change the sheets since that monumental lay. Well, I assume that was their rationale. But for all its historical resonance, the cockroaches and perpetual hum of the light fittings make me lonesome and bored, restless and homesick to the extent that I feel a compulsion to frequent a downtown singles bar, situated near a bunch of question-able looking buildings with signs over the doors that read 'French Model – Third Floor'. (It is the existence of these signs that have invariably dissuaded me from patronizing the

------

establishments. I can't think of anything more humiliating than bounding all the way up to the third floor to discover that I have to copulate with a four-inch representation of the Eiffel Tower: ha ha. And anyway, judging by the barely clad young women standing on the street-corners nearby, if the lady upstairs is a model, then I'll be damned surprised if she's ever advertised any of *my* regular products.)

I must admit that the prospect of attending a singles bar – any establishment in fact – where the clientele, myself included, may as well have the words 'Lonely Loser – Please Pour Scorn' tattooed onto our foreheads fills me with something less than a sparkling enthusiasm.

I've been told that in America, dating bars (and loneliness) are perfectly respectable aspects of day-to-day life, but I am British, which is a whole different kettle of fish. If God hadn't meant me to be repressed and glacial, He would have placed me in the womb of a family from Spain, or somewhere equally gregarious and awful. But I am a Brit! Viva anal retention!

Nonetheless, I swallow my pride and enter the club. It is a fifties theme bar (which, like all the fifties theme bars I have ever encountered, neglect the fun parts of the decade, like McCarthyism and the constant threat of nuclear holocaust, and instead concentrate on pigtails and Bobby Darin). The bobby-socked waitresses have a distracting habit of prancing onto the tables every ten minutes and miming to the blaring rock and roll music while performing immaculately timed dance routines. Consequently, the service is lousy. To bring the club up to date, however, the DJ has added a few contemporary tunes, including a song that goes 'I'm a big bomb/tick tick tick/Boom!' Astonishingly, when it gets to the 'Boom!' bit, the waitresses, before my very eyes, pretend to explode.

This is how the dating part works: you survey the numbered tables until you see someone who takes your fancy. You beckon over a waitress, and cautiously order your potential belle a $4 'Luv Bug' cocktail, before staring hopelessly at the floor debating whether or not to make a dash for it.

Three minutes later, five screaming waitresses scramble turbulently over to the lady's table clanging cow bells, and throw her a giant, blood-red cocktail with a sparkler sticking out of the top, while yelling 'Someone fancies you! Someone fancies you!' The DJ immediately stops the music, and excitedly reads out the name and table number of the suitor who, one assumes, was expecting something a tad more discreet, and everyone in the bar strains to get a good look at the pathetic girlfriendless fool. Then they leave the two in peace to get better acquainted.

I am in the bar for precisely an hour during which time nobody attempts to pick me up. Believe me, the experience of being simultaneously gauged unfavourably by a room full of ladies gloomy enough to want to attend a place like this in the first place is a brutal one. I comfort myself with the belief that being pronounced sexually attractive by a group of people who consider fifties theme bars to be the last word in razzle-dazzle is not the world's most terrible affront, but I know secretly that I am letting myself off too easily. Cultural superiority is the lowliest sanctuary of the uncomely art-movie goer.

$$\overline{9}$$

I flew into Los Angeles on United Airlines – 'The Friendlier Skies' – an airline so congenial, in fact, that the company appear to have initiated a Happy Laughter Staff Policy for all their flights.

'I'm afraid I've been put in non-smoking,' I said, while boarding.

'Ha ha ha ha ha ha,' replied the ticket collector, gaily.

'What?' I snapped.

'Do you require a smoking seat?' she sang.

'Yeees,' I replied, cautiously.

'Ha ha ha ha,' she replied, grinning and winking.

I glanced behind me for signs of an amusing thing, but there was nothing to be found, so – tentatively – I continued.

'So can I have smoking?'

'Of course,' she replied, slowly. 'Just tell the lady over there. She'll see to your needs.'

'That lady?'

'Ha ha ha ha ha ha.' And so on.

This all-pervading corporate euphoria continued throughout the journey. The in-flight safety video depicted a planeful of merry patrons gleefully placing oxygen masks over their faces, as if it were their dream come true to discover themselves in a great height crisis that required supplementary oxygen, like they were taking part in a Walt Disney oxygen mask fun party happy-smiley time.

And when I complained that the economy class seats had a leg room designed for the woman who played ET, the stewardess chuckled with mirth, and gave me a big wink. Now: I'm no sourpuss, and I like a laugh and a giggle. And if, for instance, I'd just revealed to her that my mother-in-law is so fat that whenever she falls out of bed she rolls herself back to sleep, I could have handled this response. But I was *criticising*, for God's sake. And when I criticise, I want people to react sombrely.

I got talking to the man sitting on the next seat. You meet people on planes. During the last three weeks, for instance,

I've had a Marxist who told me I was pathetic because I didn't believe in anything, I've had a multiple sclerosis sufferer who told me she was cured, just passing the time, telling stories until we land. And I tell them my stories too. On this flight, I had an old black man from Compton who'd spent a year saving $6000 from his job as a school janitor to 'invest in Las Vegas'. He lost the lot. 'Don't go there,' he said. 'Don't go. It's the land of the Devil.'

We talked about what it was like to be black in Compton, which is what you invariably end up talking about to somebody who is black and from Compton.

'There's a big explosion going on,' he said. 'If you're going to write anything, write the *truth*. I know what you're thinking. You're thinking: "How can I trust a man who smokes cocaine?" and I *do* smoke cocaine, but I'm primarily a wino. But I've got my dignity, and now that I'm asking you for money, I want you to know that it's hurting me to do this.' And so on.

'You know that explosion I was talking about,' he said.

'Yes,' I replied.

'Well when it comes – and it *will* come – it won't be racial. It'll be *financial*. Write that. It's very important that you write that.'

'Okay,' I replied. 'I will.'

I wanted to do some shopping before my drive to Vegas, and the man at the airport recommended the Universal City-walk Shopping Complex, in Ventura Boulevard, up in the hills, the North Hollywood hills that look over the city, which looks like east Manchester with exotic vegetation.

'CityWalk will have everything you need,' he said, and added – almost in a whisper, 'And it's safe.'

'Are things really that bad?'

'Times are hard,' replied the man at the airport. 'But you'll *adore* CityWalk.'

———

CityWalk is a walled shopping centre, a shopping complex under fortification, with its own armed police department whose job is to defend the wealthy shops and wealthy

———

shoppers against wrongdoers, non-commissioned buskers, street vendors and leafleteers. This is all written into their Code Of Conduct, which is displayed on walls all over the site. It's a pogrom: a great big colourful street life pogrom. I'm all for it! No buskers at CityWalk! No chestnut sellers, unicyclists, escape artists, or jugglers! No street vendors! No *Big Issue* sellers! No happy bouncy Krishnas with their complementary Krishna cookbooks!

And, joy upon joy, no Church Of Scientology Free Personality Test leafleteers! (I could never understand the attraction of the L Ron Hubbard lovers anyway. It continually amazes me that anybody who wrote such substandard sci-fi books could have been apportioned demigod status. It's like worshipping in the Church of Sidney Sheldon. Anyway, you have to ask yourself, what's so bad about their Personality Tests that they have to *give them away*. If you ask me, that's suspicious. Any decent personality test would be *costly*.)

And, yes, you can walk through the streets of CityWalk wholly unfettered by that nagging conundrum: how come all the people who hand you 'Learn To Speak English' leaflets don't know how to speak English themselves? What kind of advert is that? I'm speaking here, of course, as a somewhat biased resident of Covent Garden – an area of London where your shopping pleasure is heightened by the knowledge that, at any time, there is almost certainly an amusing mime artist standing right behind you, imitating your every movement for the entertainment of the children. You trip over a paving stone, they trip over a paving stone. You swing your bag, they swing their bag. Everyone laughs. If I ever opt for suicide – I have resolved – I'm going to do myself in at the Covent Garden Piazza. If I'm going down, I'm going to take one of these fuckers with me.

So I salute CityWalk, for they have passed a law against all these undesirables. Turn up unannounced and start hollering 'Just Like A Woman' without a permit, and the LAPD are wholly within their rights to jump on you en masse and bludgeon you into unconsciousness with their truncheons. CityWalk doesn't even stop there. Also banned are beggars, homeless people, street gangs and – I kid you not – people who wear their baseball caps the wrong way round. Their multiplex cinema refused to show the South Central LA based movie *Poetic Justice*, citing it's violence as justification for prohibiting it. But it is not a violent movie. It's far less violent than, say, *Carlito's Way* which is playing here today.

CityWalk is a commercial triumph! Residents of the Valley and Beverly Hills are flocking here in their thousands. The place has only been open for a year, and it is LA's premiere success story of the nineties. (You *do* still see black and Latino faces here from time to time, but most are carrying guttering from one half-built emporium to another.)

What exactly is it that the combined forces of the LAPD and the LASO are so effectively protecting here at CityWalk? Thirty-eight shops and restaurants, businesses like The Nature Company that sell 'Know Your Insects' t-shirts, 'Spirit Of The Forest' and 'Wolf Talk' CDs, enough glossy leaflets eulogizing the 'Wonderful World Of Bats' to evict a stadium full of Amazonian tree people. The Nature Company has a placard on its door, their corporate pledge that: 'Authenticity And Knowledge Are Balanced With Sufficient Humour To Give Our Customers An Experience Which Makes Them Feel Good About Themselves And The World In Which They Live'.

But the sign is unnecessary. Everybody here looks as if they are thoroughly content about themselves and the world in which they live.

––––

After wandering around for a while I stop for a milkshake, and get talking to Charlie, a white boy from Miami who serves at the LA Juice 'n' Salad For Fun stall.

'It must be strange working in a place with so many rules,' I say.

'There's nothing wrong with these rules,' he snaps, with surprisingly forceful defensiveness. And then he says, 'This place is very beautiful and we've got to keep it that way, whatever the cost.'

'You mean defend it against the blacks?'

'What do you mean? Who said "blacks"? I didn't say "blacks". What are you saying?'

'Sorry,' I reply. 'I've just got back from South Africa, and I guess that the blacks there are the problem, if you're a white . . .'

'Yeah, well, there's nothing wrong with the blacks here. I've got some very good black friends.'

'So who are you defending CityWalk against?'

Charlie pauses for a moment, thinks about it, and replies, 'The bad people. What we've got here is *good*.'

To show me what he's referring to he waves his hand across the panorama: past the Hollywood mountains, the rich blue skies, past Captain Coconuts with the electric parrot in the window that wolf-whistles at you as you walk past, past the World Of Magic Theatre Restaurant with the 3-D hologram tarot reader and the large gyrating carrots and bananas that dance when you clap, that open and close their mouths, as if they're singing along to the music. Charlie's hand comes to rest at the Museum Of Neon Art, the centrepiece of which is an impressive, fastidiously created one hundred per cent all-neon *Mona Lisa*.

'It's dangerous out there,' says Charlie. 'There's a lot of bad people about, and we've got to protect what's ours.'

'But I guess that all of this is for the tourists,' I reply.

'No it's not,' says Charlie. 'No it's not. It's for us.'

'The *Mona Lisa* is great,' I say.

'That's nothing,' replies Charlie. 'You haven't seen anything. Watch this.' He takes me over to the *Mona Lisa* display, claps his hands, and *Mona Lisa* winks at me.

'Wow,' I say.

'See what I mean?' says Charlie.

10

And, finally, onwards into Vegas. My few hours in Los Angeles (from CityWalk to the motorway, via lunch) had been hell: smoker hell that only smokers truly understand. The city's one, sole smoking restaurant – on Sunset Boulevard – was all but draped in black, and whenever I lit a cigarette on the street, everybody went 'phooh' and wafted the air with their hands. Of course this whole southern California health thing is a great big sham, as the case of River Phoenix – tofu dolphin by day, crazed smack spook by night – so eloquently displayed. Californians haven't given up unhealthy living: they just do it when no one's looking. And they do it in Vegas. In spades.

The dusty, solitary, misanthropic drive through the Nevada Desert I'd visualized (and hoped for) turned out to be a one-hundred-and-fifty-mile long traffic jam through ugly and morose concrete towns like Baker and Barstow. Baker was once home to the highest recorded ground temperature in the world, so they built a great towering thermometer to commemorate this achievement. Then somewhere else got hotter, and now they don't like to talk about it. Now they're just stuck with the gargantuan fucker: a perpetually mocking reminder of glorious days gone by. In fact, they don't like to talk about anything much in Baker (with one exception from the local radio DJ who – when I turned on – was informing a listener how 'great' it was that she was blind, and was, thus, compelled to listen to Desert Radio twenty-four hours a day. 'I guess TV's out of the question,' he chuckled. 'I guess we're stuck with each other.' 'Yeah,' muttered the lady with a tired whine. 'I guess we are, Big Bob.')

I was out of petrol by the time I passed through the town. My dollars were all gone, and a big sign on the gas station door said 'No Credit Cards'. Nonetheless, with barely enough petrol to get me to the next garage, I had no choice but to engage the attendent in negotiation.

'Um, excuse me,' I said. 'I'm in rather a spot of bother. I'm all out of petrol and I need enough to get me to Las Vegas. I haven't any dollars, and I see from your sign that you don't accept credit cards. However, if you'll let me have a little gas, I'll gladly give you the money when I pass by this way tomorrow.'

The attendant stared at me in stagnant silence, a tiny droplet of saliva dribbling down his chin. I waited for an answer, but he just stared.

'Soooo,' I continued, cautiously, 'if you'd let me have just a little petrol . . .'

The attendant continued to stare at me, sluggishly wiping a fly away from his mouth that obviously believed that anything that inanimate had to be a tree and was, therefore, safe to lay eggs on and drink from its sap. This time the silence lasted about a minute. I thought it best to start again.

'Um, excuse me,' I said. 'I'm in rather a spot of bother. I'm all out of petrol and I need enough to get me to Las Vegas. I haven't any dollars, and I see from your sign that you don't accept credit cards. However, if you'll let me have a little gas, I'll gladly give you the money when I pass by this way tomorrow.' I gave him a hopeful grin. The attendent scratched his forehead, idly rubbed his underarm, and stared at me.

'Hello?' I said, gingerly.

'Hi there!' replied the attendant.

'Ah,' I said, breezily. 'I'm in rather a spot of bother and I wonder if you can help me . . .' But the attendant began to chat to the person he'd just said hello to, and I threw up my arms in defeat. Eventually, my car and I limped fifteen miles to a garage that accepted the principle of credit cards, although not the principle of an outside world.

There's only two hundred and fifty miles of nothingness between the two tremendous glittering cities of Los Angeles and Las Vegas, possibly the two most famed entertainment centres in the world. Most desert communities are just two hundred and fifty miles away from more lizards. Yet, the petrol pump attendant who served me that night had all the curiosity of a cactus.

'On your way to Vegas, huh?' he said. 'We get a lot of you guys passing this way.'

'It must be handy for you,' I replied.

'Well, I don't know about that,' he said, lackadaisically. 'I've never been there myself.'

'Do you go to Los Angeles instead?'

'Nope,' he replied. 'Never been there neither.'

'So where *have* you been?'

'Well, if I need shopping done I go into Barstow, and on a Friday night, if we want to have some fun, we head on down to Jack's Tavern on the old road to Death Valley.'

Eventually, sixty miles before the Nevada state line, the traffic began to disperse and I was driving alone. The radio went off the air. All around me was nature. It was beginning to get dark, and then, suddenly, it got incredibly dark. And, miles away in the distance, a tiny light, like a firefly hummed and shot flashes into the air. And then – like being hit over head with a hammer – the light became Las Vegas.

———

Las Vegas has the second highest death rate from nicotine usage in the world. (I have no idea what the first is: but it must be a hell of a place.) They *celebrate* cancer here. The Guinness World Of Records exhibit on Las Vegas Boulevard includes a film of the Man Who Can Smoke Eighteen Cigars At Any One Time. *Eighteen*, by God! It's an astonishing, inspiring sight, and makes one wonder exactly how he chanced upon his very special talent. ('Hey! I wonder what'll happen if I put two in here. Hey, that's kinda fun. Let's try three . . .')

He appears delighted in the film, happily puffing his way into the history books. And his endeavour is rewarded by a huge, appreciative crowd gathered around the exhibit, clapping and laughing. As it turns out, I spend longer than I anticipated wandering around the Guinness World Of Records. Launching oneself into the casinos on the Strip is a daunting proposition, a voracious monster of neon and noise. As much as I hate to gamble, I love it equally, and I am doing all I can to postpone the inevitable. So, instead, I while away a pleasant evening perusing extremely tall people, extremely short people, women with beards, a man from Pennsylvania who can attract ten thousand bees to his body at any particular time, and a load of big carrots and tomatoes that aren't quite so enjoyable.

At the end of the presentation, there is a special section where young children are invited to attempt to beat a record themselves. Today, it's the most jumps of a skipping rope.

'C'mon Cindy,' urges the announcer. 'That's only sixteen. You can do better than that.'

Cindy starts to cry. 'It's okay, Cindy,' he hastily adds. 'Sixteen's fine.'

But we all know it's not. The record is about a million. Cindy exits humiliated and defeated, as indeed she should. Sixteen's shite. As I watch this display, I can't help but ponder how much more invigorating it would have been if the youngsters were asked to break the slightly more hazardous records: perhaps the cigar-smoking or bee-attracting ones. Now that would be entertainment.

'C'mon Cindy. That's just three panatellas. You can do better than that. C'mon Cindy. That's only forty wasps. Smear more honey.' I don't know: there's just something about Las Vegas that brings out the most mean-spirited aspects of one's personality.

———

There are more suicides per capita in Las Vegas than anywhere, which is why – I am informed by Danny the room service man on my arrival – they've sealed up my bedroom window on the seventh floor of the Mirage Hotel. Of course, the by-product of this is that you have to use *their* oxygen. They don't even allow you the dignity of deciding whether to inhale *their* oxygen or God's. You either use *their* oxygen or you lie on the floor going 'ach ach ach'. That's the choice. The casino management pump it into the gaming rooms with the same vicious scheming that motivates them to conceal the exit doors behind the pot plants. Once you're inside the casino, there are no clocks, no sunlight, no sleep (the oxygen sees to that), and no escape. And this is the new style Vegas, the Vegas for the children, for all the family, the Vegas envisioned and created by the richest corporate man in America, Steve Wynn. Steve is a star in Vegas.

———

Scattered all across the Strip are Steve's dreams made reality: immense gaudy pretend volcanos that explode at fifteen minute intervals, pretend pirate battles with pretend parrots, pretend lions and huge, tawdry pretend zebras. And the fun doesn't stop there: channels seventeen and eighteen of the hotel's TV are set aside for a promotional movie about a little boy who goes – with his parents – to stay at the Treasure Island Hotel, and while mom and dad are checking in, the little boy gets approached by our hero in the foyer.

'Your adventure is only just beginning,' says Steve, clicking his fingers, and the little boy is magically transformed into a rabid, uncontrollable gambling addict. I'm kidding, of course. The little boy is actually magically transformed into a swash-buckling pirate.

'When I was a little boy, I wanted to be a pirate,' yells the child, sweetly.

'I'll tell you a secret,' replies Steve with as much sweetness as he can muster (this is a man, mind you, who looks more at home saying things like 'Luca Brazi sleeps with the fishes' than 'Come and play in Never-Never Land', so we're not talking about a truckload of sweetness here).

'I'll tell you a secret,' he says. 'I wanted to be a pirate too.' And, hell, congratulations, Steve. Your dream came true.

It is only when you witness a society *this* impure that you truly value the virtue of purity. As I wander down the strip, passing hordes of sobbing, terrified children overdosing on the sheer magnitude of the fun, I feel a desperate, overwhelming urge to stroke kittens and buy Garfield posters that say 'I Hate Monday Mornings' and read the *Mail On Sunday* so I can look at the back page photograph of two baby giraffes cuddling up, and feel warm inside. I need comfort and reassurance. I am ripe for the picking: so much so, in fact, that I have to stop myself from rushing to the casino's Redemption Stall, and beg for absolution. Which is lucky really. The Redemption Stall is the place where you cash your chips.

As more and more states across America are opening themselves up for gambling business, Steve Wynn's plan is to redefine Vegas as a city of fun for all the family. So, while the kids are playing pirates and dad is squandering the life savings on Caribbean Stud Poker, mom can peruse the newly built high-class shopping precincts and purchase such fabulous gifts as t-shirts emblazoned with gold falcons in flight, mock-Fabergé eggs, and, well, t-shirts emblazoned with gold falcons in flight and mock-Fabergé eggs.

Up at the MGM Grand, you can play craps while hobnobbing with your favourite characters from the *Wizard Of Oz*: the Tin Man gazing over your shoulder for good luck, kissing the dice.

'Your job must be fun,' I say to Dorothy, as she's heading for her break.

'I just want to go home,' she replies, wistfully.

'And me,' I say.

'Are you from Kansas too?' she sings, chuckling.

'Cut the crap,' I reply. 'How long have you been Dorothy?'

'Just two weeks,' she says. 'The last Dorothy had to leave.'

'What happened to her?'

She comes up close to me and whispers, 'She got addicted to the slot machines. She spent eight hours a day going around singing, "Because Because Because Because Becaaaause . . ." and the rest of the time she was pumping hundreds of dollars into the machines.'

'So Dorothy finally surrendered.'

'I'm a bit worried about the Lion,' confides Dorothy. 'His name's Frank. He's getting badly into the Stud Poker.'

'Well at least he found his courage,' I reply.

Dorothy shrugs. 'I guess so,' she says.

———

Dorothy and I get talking, and we go for coffee at the Burger King – Vegas is the only place I've visited where you have to dive into a fast food restaurant to eschew the tastelessness. We agree – Dorothy and I – that the kiddie thing is terrifying, not to mention wholly misplaced in a town created to destroy the lives of the weak, the whole experience being not unlike visiting an opium den where the chief pipe-filler is Yosemite Sam. I tell Dorothy about my hotel window being sealed up to stop me from throwing myself out, and she tells me a story in return.

———

It's a long story and she tells it with vigour – she obviously wanted the opportunity to tell someone, even though she isn't an extrovert. (She keeps saying that. 'I'm not an extrovert. This Judy Garland thing is just a job. I'm just *pretending* to be an extrovert.') But its a long story, so I'll cut to the important part.

She was living with her boyfriend in Salt Lake City. They were happy. But one night, he invited his ex-girlfriend over for supper. It was the first time Dorothy had met her, and she turned out to be beautiful and funny.

'Don't you hate it when that happens,' asks Dorothy.

'I hate that,' I agree.

Anyway, the ex-girlfriend kept on saying terribly witty things, talking back to the TV, that sort of thing. So Dorothy sat there in silence, feeling insecure and defective. And the more silent she became, the more inadequate she felt. It got to the stage where she never thought she'd say another thing in her life, while her boyfriend and his ex were laughing and chatting.

After the ex went home, Dorothy's boyfriend turned to her, gave her a huge kiss, and said: 'You were so wonderful just now. I loved you so much tonight. You were sitting there so at ease, so confident. And I looked over to you and loved you for it.' And Dorothy thought to herself: 'Wow! That was a lucky break!' Then she thought: 'Hang on. How could he have got it *that wrong*? Doesn't he *know* me?' So she left him and moved to Vegas and got this job. While she tells me this story, she plays with her pigtails and her little blue and white dress. Then she goes back to work and I start gambling.

———

It is 6.00 a.m. on the second day when I finally make it outside. The sun is beginning to rise, but it is overcast. My plan had been to play blackjack for maybe two hours, and then head off to see Joel's boy give his performance. Of course, I missed the whole thing.

While I was inside the casino, I got chatting to a man who divulged to me the secret of successful blackjack playing, which consisted of memorizing the cards played by associating

———

each with a particular everyday action. For example, the six of clubs is walking down the street. The king of hearts is going into a grocery store. The four of diamonds is buying an apple, and so on. Once you have all the cards memorized, and you've reached the end of the pack, you can be pretty certain whether the dealer will pull a high or a low card. And once you know that, you will have the advantage of knowing whether to twist or stick.

By 3.00 a.m., I was sitting in a hardware shop precariously balancing four oranges, a pomegranate, a copy of the Bible, and nine sparrows in my arms. My hands were full, so I had to put down the oranges to pick up the six spanners. Of course, I dropped the lot, and while I scrambled desperately around on the floor to retrieve my items, four Spaniards and a Scrabble board whisked past my head, crashing against the back wall. By this time, I was so lost in the corridors of the hardware store, so far away from the blackjack table, that I pulled a jack with a hand of seventeen, and everybody tutted at me. It was a bad night.

———

Now, out on the street where – last night – clusters of pimps were handing out 'Actual Photographs Of Nude Entertainers – Direct To Your Room', there are groups of Jesus people, offering Jesus Magazines, magazines called *Awake* and *Alive*, inviting passers-by to pray with them.

'How much did you lose?' asks a nice woman called Gillian.

'$450,' I mumble.

'Do you believe in Jesus?' she says.

'Um,' I reply.

'For every dollar you lost, Jesus shed a tear,' she says.

'Did he?'

'Would you like to pray with us?' she says. 'We can pray right now.'

'Here?' I reply, startled. 'Here on the pavement. With all the cars going by?'

'Jesus doesn't mind where you pray,' she says. 'Come on. Let's pray. Let's pray now. Right now.'

———

'Yes,' agrees her companion, hastily. 'Let's go pray.'

'We can pray in the car park if you feel shy,' says Gillian.

'In the car park of the Mirage Hotel?' I ask, shocked.

'Yes,' she says. 'Let us pray together.'

They take me to an empty spot not far from the road, near the courtesy taxi queue, near the placard erected by Steve Wynn in homage to Siegfried and Roy, the hotel's resident magic entertainers who make elephants and tigers disappear, that sort of thing, '. . . As The Pioneers Of Family Entertainment In Las Vegas, They Have Changed The Course Of History. Furthermore, They Have Made Conservation History In Providing Tireless Leadership To Help Preserve Nature's Endangered White Tigers . . .'.

'Oh Lord, I ask you to pray for . . .' (pause)

'Jon.'

'. . . Jon's soul, for he is lost in the wilderness, addicted to gambling . . .'

'Steady on.'

'. . . He needs your love and guidance, Lord, he needs to be rescued from the clutches of Satan . . .'

'. . . Let's not get carried away here . . .'

'. . . In Jesus's name. Amen.'

'Amen.'

Then some more people join us: some Jehovah's Witnesses who happen to be walking past. And – before I know it – I'm surrounded by a big bunch of thrilled Christians, gazing at their latest convert with pride, almost poking me with delight.

'Would you like to make a donation?' says one.

'Come and help us sell our papers,' says another.

'Give us a "J . . ." ' yells yet another, and the whole group hollers 'J . . .'. And so on.

Unfortunately, in her early morning thrill of successfully enrolling a new zealot, the poor lady gets some of the letters the wrong way round, which – as you can imagine – could've been disastrous at the 'put it together and what have we got' part. But – praise be! – when we DO finally make it to that section, everyone yells out 'JESUS' and not 'JSESU', which doesn't have quite the same ring.

The morning progresses, and the Christians (with *me* in tow) walk up and down the strip screaming at the pimps. *'Perverts!'* yell Gillian. *'Disgusting creeps!'*

'Repent!' screams Gillian's friend, Melissa.

'Have we asked you for a donation yet?' says Gillian. 'Oh we did? Oh.'

'Were you raised a Christian?' asks Melissa.

'I was raised a Jew,' I reply.

'That's okay,' says Melissa swiftly. 'That's really absolutely fine.'

'Jesus loves Jews too,' says Gillian. 'We're *especially* happy to meet Jews.' And they both quickly nod.

It begins to rain, just a few spots, but Gillian holds her hand out to catch the drops.

'The floods are coming,' she exclaims, and they all laugh.

'What's that?' I say.

'It's just a joke we have,' she replies, blushing a little.

'Whenever it rains out here in the desert, that is what we say: "The floods are coming. The floods are coming. Let's round up the animals".'

It's time for me to go, so I thank them for their hospitality.

'Any time,' they said. 'Take care of yourself on your journey home.'

'I will,' I reply. 'And when I'm on the motorway, I promise I won't look back. I won't look over my shoulder.'

'You're not out of the wilderness yet,' says Melissa. 'Vegas may be Sodom, but Los Angeles is Gomorrah.'

'Goodbye,' I say.

'Bless you,' says Melissa, which is odd, because I hadn't sneezed.

Acknowledgements

Special thanks go to Trevor Dolby and Emma Lawson at Pavilion, Carol Chamberlain, Jill, Lynn and Julia for research, Vivienne Clore at the Richard Stone Partnership, David Quantick for giving me the Eugene Terre'Blanche *Hobbit* joke, Dominic Wells at *Time Out* for letting me reproduce relevant bits of past columns, Mike and Lindy Gunn at the excellent Gunn's Camp in the Okavango Delta, Martin Vincent, Rachel Purnell, Neil Crombie and Cathy Mahoney for advice, and all the Welsh Ronsons. More information about Cecil Rhodes can be found in Brian Roberts' wonderful *Cecil Rhodes – Flawed Colossus* (Norton).